Sharpshooting
in the
Civil War

D1611228

This book is dedicated to the sharpshooters of the American Civil War, including those of both the Confederacy and the Union. No matter their uniforms, these elite marksmen served with honor, distinction, and courage.

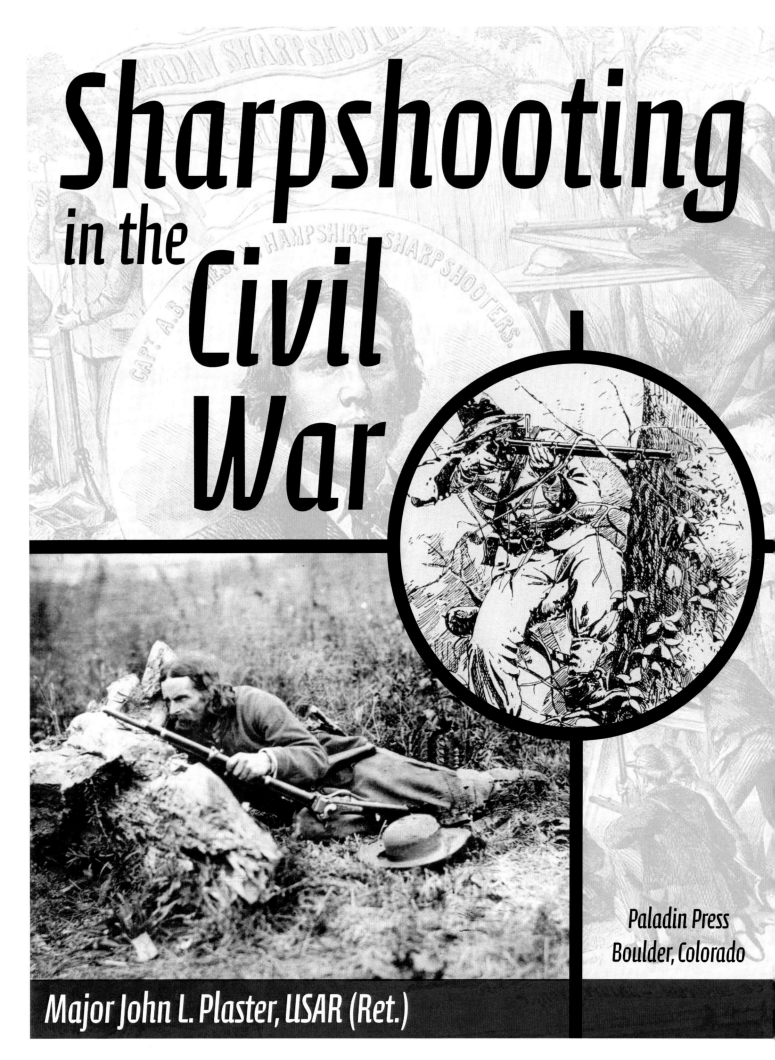

Sharpshooting
in the
Civil War

Paladin Press
Boulder, Colorado

Major John L. Plaster, USAR (Ret.)

Also by John L. Plaster
Advanced Ultimate Sniper (video)
The History of Sniping and Sharpshooting
Secret Commandos: Behind Enemy Lines with the Elite Warriors of SOG
SOG: A Photo History of the Secret Wars
SOG: The Secret Wars of America's Commandos in Vietnam
The Ultimate Sniper: An Advanced Training Manual for Military and Police Snipers
Ultimate Sniper: The Video

Sharpshooting in the Civil War
by Major John L. Plaster, USAR (ret.)

Copyright © 2009 by John L. Plaster

ISBN 13: 978-1-58160-703-1
Printed in the United States of America

Published by Paladin Press, a division of
Paladin Enterprises, Inc.
Gunbarrel Tech Center
7077 Winchester Circle
Boulder, Colorado 80301 USA, +1.303.443.7250

Direct inquiries and/or orders to the above address.

PALADIN, PALADIN PRESS, and the "horse head" design
are trademarks belonging to Paladin Enterprises and
registered in United States Patent and Trademark Office.

All rights reserved. Except for use in a review, no
portion of this book may be reproduced, stored in or
introduced into a retrieval system, or transmitted in any
form without the express written permission of the publisher.
The scanning, uploading, and distribution of this book by the
Internet or any other means without the permission of the
publisher is illegal and punishable by law. Please respect the
author's rights and do not participate in any form of electronic
piracy of copyrighted material.

Neither the author nor the publisher assumes
any responsibility for the use or misuse of
information contained in this book.

Table of Contents

Introduction 1

PART ONE: Organizing for War 3
1: Sharpshooters of the Confederacy 5
2: Sharpshooters of the Union 21

PART TWO: Sharpshooter Weapons and Tactics 39
3: Confederate Sharpshooter Weapons and Equipment 41
4: Union Sharpshooter Weapons and Equipment 59
5: Sharpshooter Tactics and Techniques 75

PART THREE: Sharpshooters in Battle 105
6: Bloody Days: Antietam and Fredericksburg 107
7: Three Days at Gettysburg 119
8: Vicksburg to the Bitter End 133

Bibliography 145

Index 149

Acknowledgments

Many people and institutions assisted my research, and contributed information and visual images. The first person I must thank is my wife, Gail, for her unending support and her considerable photographic skills. Other photographers and photo processors included Doug Black, Roger Kennedy, and Charles Farrow. The book's original art flowed from the talented pen of Tami Anderson.

Many other individuals and institutions contributed to this book, among them:

American Precision Museum Association

Archives of Michigan, Ms. Julie K. Meyerle

Augusta (Georgia) Historical Society

Bureau County (Illinois) Historical Society

Chickamauga-Chattanooga National Military Park, Mr. Jim Ogden

Columbus (Georgia) City Museum

Congressional Medal of Honor Society, Ms. Beverly VanValkenburg

Detroit Institute of Arts Founders Society, Ms. Beth Garfield

Mr. Dan P. Fagen

Historic Publications Co., Mr. William H. Hastings

Historical Society of Pennsylvania, Ms. Amy Fleming

Mr. Garry James

Mr. Chuck Karwan

Ms. Eulane Matthews

Michigan History Museum

Mr. John Milius

Minnesota Historical Society

Museum of the Confederacy, Ms. Malinda W. Collier

National Firearms Museum, Mr. Doug Wickland

National Infantry Museum, Fort Benning, Georgia, Mr. Z. Frank Hanner

National Museum of American History, Smithsonian Institution, Ms. Sarah J. Rittgers

National Rifle Association

Oneida Nation Museum, Ms. Nadine Escamea

Public Affairs Office, Fort Benning, Georgia

Springfield Armory National Historical Site

State Historical Society of Wisconsin, Mr. Andy Krushaar

Tennessee State Library and Archives

Mr. Don Troiani, Southbury, Connecticut

University of Minnesota Libraries

U.S. Army Center of Military History

U.S. Army Military History Institute

U.S. National Park Service, with special thanks to the staffs at Gettysburg, Petersburg, and Vicksburg
    National Military Parks

Vermont Historical Society, Mr. Paul Carnahan

Virginia Historical Society, Ms. Ann Marie Price

Virginia Museum of Fine Arts, Richmond

West Point Museum, Mr. Robert W. Fisch, Curator of Arms

Introduction

This is the first full-length book that focuses exclusively on Civil War sharpshooting—the men, along with their weapons, tactics, training, organization, and operations—and it represents more than two decades of research. It relies on virtually thousands of sources, from newspaper articles, unit histories and diaries, to letters in monthly issues of *Confederate Veteran* magazine, along with surveys of several battlefields. Though no history can claim to be complete, it is as thorough and detailed as I could make it.

It was well worth the effort, considering that this was the first major conflict in which both armies had rifles as their primary armament. Ignoring how this impacted on an infantryman's range and lethality, the prevailing Napoleonic tactics often created situations ideal for sharpshooting. For these mistakes, the leaders, too, suffered—never before or since would so many officers—especially general officers—fall victim to deliberate, well-placed shots.

Ironically, despite their great skill, few sharpshooters were formally trained, both armies largely relying on self-learned, prewar marksmen. In the South, most sharpshooters came from rural, hunting backgrounds, while their Northern counterparts (at least initially) were competitive shooters who brought along their own target rifles. Regardless, most were volunteers and worthy of the title "elite." My greatest satisfaction in telling this story came from rediscovering heroic but forgotten sharpshooters who'd slipped into the dusty cracks of history.

And they were a true elite. "The giving of these telescopic rifles . . . was in the nature of a mark of honor," explained the Berdan Sharpshooters unit history, "as the sharpshooter thus armed was considered an independent character, used only for special service, with the privilege of going to any part of the line where in his own judgment he could do the most good."

On the downside, however, they lived hazardous lives; for ordinary soldiers often considered them killers, grim reapers who coolly harvested lives from afar without fair warning. As a Civil War journalist observed, sharpshooters were "not likely very often to be taken prisoners, as death is considered their just penalty; for as they very seldom are in a position to show mercy, so, in like manner, is mercy rarely shown them."

Yet, there can be little question of their overall effectiveness. In his seminal work, *Regimental Losses in the American Civil War*, Lieutenant Colonel William F. Fox reported, "Berdan's United States Sharp-Shooters . . . undoubtedly killed more men than any other regiment in the army. In skirmishing they had no equal." This was likely so for Confederate sharpshooter units, as well.

If you enjoy this book, you'll undoubtedly appreciate the much larger volume from which it is derived, *The History of Sniping and Sharpshooting*. Also by Paladin Press, it traces the subject from the French and Indian War of the 1750s to the modern battlefields of Iraq and Afghanistan.

John L. Plaster

May 2009

1 ORGANIZING FOR WAR

CHAPTER ONE

Sharpshooters of the Confederacy

The American Civil War stands as a demarcation, a crossing point from wars of old to wars of the new mechanical age. For the first time, whole armies could be moved by steamboat and supplied by railroad; ironclad gunboats patrolled hostile rivers and shores; telegraphs instantly dispatched orders and intelligence; and men were shot down by telescopically sighted rifles so far away that their comrades never heard the muzzle report.

This was also the world's first conflict with entire armies of contending riflemen. Unappreciative of rifle capabilities—their improved accuracy, range, and rate of fire—officers on both sides deployed infantry in shoulder-to-

Despite their rifles' considerable range, Civil War infantry often fought in shoulder-to-shoulder rows, little changed from the Revolutionary War.

The first general officer from either side to die in the Civil War, Confederate General Robert Garnett is shot by a sharpshooter, 13 July 1861.

shoulder rows, unchanged from the days of Washington. For these mistakes, the leaders, too, suffered. Fighting well forward in such compressed battlefields, never before or since would so many officers—especially general officers—fall victim to the well-placed shots of sharpshooters.

At the beginning of the war, it was uncertain what exactly constituted a Civil War sharpshooter. Classically, any rifleman fit the definition by virtue of his rifle's range exceeding that of the smooth-bore musket and his ability to engage targets selectively. But now, with all infantrymen armed with rifles, defining a sharpshooter solely by his armament had become moot.

This was equally true for unit designations. Alleged sharpshooter units popped up like mushrooms after a summer rain: scanning Confederate and Union records yields nearly 50 organizations of varying sizes—from independent companies to entire regiments—called "sharpshooters." Most such units had no selection criteria beyond the soldier's readiness to enlist. Some units assumed this label from a sense of pride, others as a recruiting tool, and only a few as an accurate indicator of function, capabilities, and mission.

In the case of South Carolina's "Palmetto Sharpshooters," although originally mustered as a genuine sharpshooter unit, a senior officer later wrote that "the exigencies of the army prevented the consummation of this design," and they were employed as conventional infantry and rarely as sharpshooters. The Union Army, too, had problems, exemplified by the attempt to form a sharpshooter unit to help defend Morris Island, South Carolina. Instead of receiving the master riflemen that local units were ordered to provide him, the unit's commander, Captain T.B. Brooks, observed, "The present so-

Sharpshooters Against Ships

Possessing a decisively larger fleet, the Union Navy blockaded the South to cut off supplies from Europe and to slice apart the Confederacy along major rivers. Control these waterways, it was believed, and the rebellion would wither away.

Confident in their superiority, Union ironclads initially left their decks and wheelhouses unprotected from small arms fire—and here was a vulnerability. Rebel sharpshooters flocked to bluffs and shorelines to take shots at these unwary naval passersby, sometimes with considerable success.

On 21 June 1861, the Union Navy's seven-ship Potomac Bay flotilla, commanded by Commander James H. Ward, landed troops on the Virginia shore to attack a Rebel artillery battery. One of the Navy's brightest senior officers, Ward had been a founding instructor at Annapolis and the author of several books on strategy and modern technology. Aboard his flagship, the *Thomas Freeborn*, a side-wheel ironclad, Ward soon realized the attack had failed and ordered a withdrawal. Bringing his ship near shore to cover the extraction, Ward left the bridge to sight the *Freeborn*'s bow gun and was shot dead by a Confederate sharpshooter, the first naval officer of either side to die in the war.

The first naval officer to die in the Civil War, Union Navy Commander James Ward was shot by a Rebel sharpshooter while aboard the USS Freeborn.

Every time a Union ship ventured into a Southern river, it faced the possibility of sharpshooter fire, sometimes causing no more than a metallic hailstorm when bullets splattered into its protective hull. Other times, caught unaware, Union officers walking the deck or observing through binoculars were picked off one after another. "Once in a while the top of a man's head would rise above the bulkhead and a body shot would be received by an unfortunate Yank that chanced to show his head above what we called the 'dead' line," wrote one former sharpshooter.

Even when no one was visible aboard a Yankee ship, Rebel sharpshooters demonstrated their skill by ringing ships' bells or hitting materiel targets. Confederate sharpshooter Tom Hall recalled "shooting the sights off the big guns on the gunboats. Every day we could see the brass shine a mile off, and whenever we were sure one could be 'tripped' the crack of an Enfield would ring merrily over the water, and away would fly a valuable piece of Yankee property."

Union gunboats fired back, of course, but often with little effect. "In the entire five weeks that our squad was fighting gunboats," sharpshooter Hall reported, "only three of us were hurt, and they were caught by a big limb that a Yankee shell knocked off a tree."

Such was not always the case. On Virginia's James River, Lieutenant Davis Constable on the USS *Naugatuck* had identified a sharpshooter's position, but every time he attempted to return fire with his own rifle, the Reb dropped from sight. The clever sailor had a deck gun trained on the spot and waited for the shooter to reemerge. "Sure enough," he wrote, "when the fellow saw me standing without a rifle in my hand he again thrust the muzzle of his rifle through the bush, but before he could pull the trigger I raised my hand. 'Bang!' went the 12-pounder, and when the smoke cleared away, rebel, gun and all had been destroyed."

In several instances, Confederate sharpshooters were instrumental in the capture of Union picket ships and gunboats. On 20 January 1863, sharpshooters aboard the CSA's *Josiah A. Bell* in the Gulf of Mexico repeatedly swept the decks of the Union picket ship, USS *Morning Light*, forcing her to strike her colors. The following May on Mississippi's Yazoo River, the Union ironclad *Petrel*, with 80 men and eight guns, was sub-▶

Confederate sharpshooters snipe at a passing Union gunboat.

A sharpshooter's view of a Union ironclad on Virginia's James River.

Unprotected against small-arms fire, the crew of a Union gunboat prepares to fire a deck gun.

jected to similar fire. "In less than a minute every living soul visible on or near the boat at the opening of the fire was swept away, killed or wounded," reported the *Charleston Mercury* newspaper. While a boarding party swam furiously to seize her, sharpshooters drove the pilot from the wheel, leaving the USS *Petrel* uncontrolled and, momentarily, in Rebel hands.

Such close-run things did not always succeed. In September 1863, the Union Navy put 75 sharpshooters aboard the USS *Clifton* and 30 more on the USS *Sachem* to suppress Rebel batteries at the mouth of the Sabine River, on the Louisiana-Texas border as part of a larger landing. A lucky Confederate artillery shot struck the *Sachem*, tearing away the iron plate from the sharpshooters and scalding many with live steam. Just then the *Clifton* ran aground, and artillery pummeled her helpless hull. Both ships were lost, and with that an important reality reinforced: sharpshooters, too, had their limits.

Riflemen aboard a Federal side-wheeler pick off a Rebel sharpshooter.

Despite 100 sharpshooters on their decks, the USS Sachem *(left) and* Clifton *succumb to enemy fire at Sabine Pass, Texas.*

called sharpshooters are inefficient. First, they are not good shots; second, their arms are not in good condition; third, they are not in sufficient numbers; and fourth, they are not properly officered."

Even genuine sharpshooters often did not belong to designated sharpshooter units. Many infantry regiments pulled respected marksmen from the ranks—akin to "chosen riflemen" of earlier wars or "designated riflemen" of the 20th century—and then employed them as skirmishers, scouts, pickets, and sharpshooters within their regiment. Some such sharpshooter detachments were permanent, others only manned when a specific tactical need arose. It was how well these men performed—*how well they shot*—that made them sharpshooters. When the Union commander at the Battle of Cheat Mountain, West Virginia, found a need for sharpshooters, he pooled the best riflemen from seven Indiana and Ohio infantry regiments into a temporary detachment whose victims included a senior officer on General Robert E. Lee's staff. Not only was Lieutenant Colonel John A. Washington so well regarded that he shared a tent with Lee (who grieved his loss), but he was George Washington's great-great-grand nephew and the last family member to own the Mount Vernon estate.

Similarly, it was a temporarily appointed sharpshooter who killed Confederate General Robert S. Garnett on 13 July 1861 at Corrick's Ford, Virginia. A former commandant of cadets at West Point and the man who'd designed the Great Seal of the State of California, Garnett was the first general officer of either side to die, and much was made of it in newspapers.

This Rebel sharpshooter and his enormous rifle were captured in April 1861 along the Potomac, over which he presumably intended to snipe.

In both armies, there was little formal marksmanship training—and absolutely no sharpshooter training—with higher priority accorded to properly reloading "by the numbers" and maneuvering on command. A rifleman's shooting skills most often had been acquired before he enlisted.

And when it came to weapons, by far, most sharpshooters fired their regular assigned 1861 Springfield or 1853 Enfield rifles or their clones, accurate to 250 yards against individual targets and perhaps 500 yards in the hands of a skilled marksman firing prone or from support.

Yet there were a select few who fit the modern definition of a sharpshooter and met the highest marksmanship standards. These were sharpshooters in the truest sense.

One Newspaper's Crusade

Following the catastrophic deaths of CSA Generals Ben McCulloch and James McIntosh at Elkhorn Tavern and the "grevious" losses of Confederate officers just weeks later at the Battle of Kernstown, the *Charleston Mercury* used its editorial pages to urge the South to field units of specially trained sharpshooters. The *Mercury* correctly speculated on 27 March 1862 the following:

> "It will be found, sooner or later, that the Yankees have organized in each army a band of practiced sharpshooters, whose business it is, with long-range rifles, to pick off the officers. By means of telescopic sights, this can be done at a great distance, and where the sharpshooter himself is entirely out of danger. All he has to do is to put his rifle at rest, adjust his telescope, and shoot down officer after officer."

A month later, on 1 May 1862, the *Mercury*'s editors followed up, observing in a frustrated tone:

> "There is no excuse for the absence of a regular corps of sharpshooters from our armies. We have an abundance of the finest marksmen in the world, men practiced in the use of the rifle from early boyhood. Here was one advantage over the enemy. He had to train his, keep them long in camps of instruction, and practicing daily from rests. And yet they have the start of us, and have reaped murderous advantages. Still, we can beat the enemy in this game. The number of crack shots in our armies vastly outnumber his, and, besides being more intrepid, they have no equals at offhand firing. With these three very decided advantages, if even now we organize companies of sharpshooters, we can, as before remarked, beat the enemy in this game."

Though many such fine riflemen indeed existed in Confederate ranks and they often were employed as sharpshooters, the *Mercury*'s call for actual units of specially selected sharpshooters would go unheeded for two full years, until the spring of 1864.

CONFEDERATE SHARPSHOOTER UNITS

Like their Northern counterparts, it's impossible to generalize about the Confederate Army's sharpshooter structure early in the war. From the opening clashes onward, virtually every Southern infantry regiment employed sharpshooters with the same variety of official, unofficial, designated, undesignated, temporary, and permanent status as did the Union Army. Some units alleging to be sharpshooters actually were only skirmishers, while some companies operating as sharpshooters were called skirmishers.

Despite this variation, there was a fairly uniform result: almost every major battle included Southern sharpshooters whose well-aimed shots influenced the outcome. "It was the duty of the sharpshooters," one Virginia veteran explained simply, "to be in front in an advance and in the rear in retreat, creeping and running from shelter to shelter, always on the lookout for a good shot."

Sometimes their presence was officially cited. On 28 April 1862, Major General John Magruder reported that his right wing of the Army of the Peninsula included "four companies armed with long-range guns, and constitute the only corps of sharpshooters." That same month at Yorktown, Virginia, the 1st Texas Voluntary Infantry Regiment was called on "to provide sharpshooters to harass Yankee scouts and skirmishers who closely approached the Confederate works." This 200-man detachment existed for several months and "operated beyond and independently of the regular pickets, and soon became a terror to the enemy." A year later a similar battalion of Texas sharpshooters was formed under "the popular and charismatic" Captain Ike Turner, later killed, ironically, by a Union sharpshooter "while standing on top of the breastworks" near Suffolk, Virginia.

THE EARLY BATTLES

Going back to the war's opening days discloses an almost childish naiveté about sharpshooting, even among senior leaders. The *New York Herald* reported that Union Army Commander in Chief George McClellan "looks with abhorrence upon the barbarous practice of the shooting of pickets, which he regards as murder, and has strictly forbidden." Did he actually expect Confederate sharp-

General Nathaniel Lyon disregards an aide's warning, riding forward with his troops—right into a sharpshooter's bullet.

To their utter bewilderment, Union soldiers fighting on several fronts reported encounters with the strangest sharpshooters ever to serve the Confederacy—African Americans. The number of incidents and variety of witnesses are too great to ignore.

The unit history of Berdan's Sharpshooters, published in 1892, includes an encounter during the Yorktown Siege in 1862 with a "Negro sharpshooter" who was "a good shot at long range." The history reports that "a rebellious black made his appearance by the side of an officer and under his direction commenced firing at us." Initially the Berdan men did not fire back, purposely to embolden him. "This was what our men wanted, to get him within more reasonable range," the book explains. Eventually, Sergeant William G. Andrews of Company E, "with the aid of a fine telescope," spotted the African American sharpshooter "firing through the hole in the back of a fireplace." Andrews shot him dead "and thus ended his sport with his life."

Frederick Kirkland, a Union soldier who fought at Yorktown, similarly reported an African American Rebel sharpshooter, whose "habit was to perch himself in a big tree and keeping himself hid behind the body, [shoot] among the Union men by firing up them."

"There are among the rebel sharpshooters, a large number of Negroes," the *New York Herald* announced on 27 April 1862, "who show a good deal of ability in the use of the rifle—in fact, our pickets declare that the best shot among them is a 'darkey,' who climbs the inside of the chimney of a recently burnt house, and knocking out a brick for a porthole, sits perched inside watching his chance of a shot at our people." Originating from Yorktown, this dispatch could have been describing the same enemy sharpshooter killed by Sergeant Andrews.

Perhaps the least-recognized Civil War soldier: the black Confederate sharpshooter. (Original art by Tami Anderson.)

Professor Ervin L. Jordan Jr., author of *Black Confederates and Afro-Yankees in Civil War Virginia*, wrote, "I know of black Confederate sharpshooters who saw combat during the 1862 Seven Days Campaign." Jordan essentially verifies the time and place of the previously cited incidents. But there were more.

In his memoirs, Lieutenant Albert Jewett of the 4th New Hampshire Regiment recalled a black sharpshooter, "a remarkable marksman, located somewhere about Ft. Wagner," in South Carolina. "This man was more dreaded than almost everything else that opposed us, for his aim seemed as unerring as fate, anywhere within range of his rifle." According to Jewett, this sharpshooter could hit Union artillerymen a half mile away. "One morning soon after we had reached the front, and I had stationed my sharpshooters (about thirty of them usually) I noticed one of them, a mere boy, perhaps seventeen, who was loading his rifle in a seeming hurry." Thinking he'd spotted the black sharpshooter, the lad fired a shot and then put his eye to a peek-hole to see the result. "At the same instant the peculiar report of the rebel marksman reached me and the poor Western boy fell dead, with a bullet through his brain." Jewett never knew what happened to that black sharpshooter.

After his unit received a few well-aimed shots, Private John W. Haley, 17th Maine Infantry, wrote, "Mr. Reb made his whereabouts known, but he was so covered with leaves that no eye could discern him. Our sharpshooter drew a bead on him and something dropped, that something being a six-foot Negro whose weight wasn't less than 300 pounds."

Private James G. Bates of the 13th Indiana Volunteer Infantry wrote his father while fighting near Suffolk, Virginia,

This depiction of armed African American Confederate pickets, "seen by one of our officers through his field glasses" at Fredericksburg, was published in Harper's Weekly, *10 January 1863.*

in April–May 1863. "I can assure you of a certainty that the rebels have Negro soldiers in their army," he insisted. "One of their best sharpshooters, and the boldest of them all here, is a Negro. He dug himself a rifle pit last night [16 April] just across the river and has been annoying our pickets opposite him very much today. You can see him plainly enough with the naked eye . . . and with a spy-glass there is no mistaking him."

Bates is backed up by another 13th Indiana witness who found duplicity in a black sharpshooter after several Indianans were hit. It was not unusual for slaves to be observed digging positions or performing chores for white Confederates, so Union soldiers usually did not fire at them, considering them noncombatants. The Indianans, however, kept having men shot by a sharpshooter that their keenest observers could not detect. "But at last a Negro was observed walking leisurely along the works of the enemy," this account reveals. "He carried in his arms a long fence rail which he carelessly threw across the sand bag in front of him, and then suddenly disappeared from view. In a moment the crack of the rifle was heard, and one of the Indiana boys fell over dead, being shot through the forehead. Our hero now concluded that the Negro was a black rebel, that he was the man who had played such dreadful havoc . . . and that the harmless looking fence rail contained a murderous gun."

Holt Collier, hunter, guide, respected resident of Greenville, Mississippi—and a former Confederate sharpshooter.

Outside Vicksburg, at Chickasaw Bayou, credible witnesses reported an African American Confederate sharpshooter. In the first day's assault, on 30 December 1862, Colonel John B. Wyman, commander of the 13th Illinois Infantry Regiment, "a brave and gallant officer," was allegedly shot and killed by a black Confederate sharpshooter, according to the *New York Herald*. "On our right a Negro sharpshooter had been observed whose exploits are deserving of notice," wrote Thomas Knox, the paper's correspondent. "He mounts a breastwork regardless of all danger, and getting sight of a Federal soldier, draws up his musket at arm's length and fires, never failing of hitting his mark. . . . It is certain that Negroes are fighting here, though probably only as sharpshooters."

General George H. Gordon of the Union Army similarly reported, "Many men from my command were killed, and strange stories bruited about of the precision fire of a negro marksman, a Rebel."

Were these cases of mistaken identity? Sometimes, yes. At the Battle of Williamsburg, Edward Small of the 2nd New Hampshire Volunteers, spotted a black sharpshooter and fired. "I hit that fellow in the head, and he was black enough to be a Negro," he called. The next day, indeed, a dead sharpshooter was found at the place indicated by Small—*but he was an Indian*. A considerable number of North Carolina Indians had joined the Rebel cause; perhaps some had intermarried with African Americans or naturally had dark complexions. This could well account for some "black sharpshooters."

But the number of incidents well away from North Carolina is too great for so pat an answer. The mystery, then, is motivation: why would a black man have fought for the Confederate cause? Since these black sharpshooters were encountered only as lone shooters, it's possible that they fought as individual freemen, superb marksmen who sold their shooting services—essentially, paid mercenaries.

That may be true for some, but I think the more likely explanation is found in the experience of Holt Collier, the only black Confederate sharpshooter I can actually put a name to. A hunting guide, he was made famous in 1902 when his hunter client, President Theodore Roosevelt, refused to shoot a restrained bear—igniting the national craze for "teddy bears. Roosevelt found the former slave a decent man who had "all the dignity of an African chief." How, then, had he fought for the Confederacy? "In the Civil War," Roosevelt explained, "he had not only followed his master to battle as his body-servant, but had acted under him as a sharpshooter against the Union soldiers."

On 28 February 2004, the Veterans Administration provided a Confederate headstone that was ceremoniously placed atop Collier's previously unmarked grave—to commemorate Mississippi's only officially recognized Confederate soldier of African descent and, as residents still say, one of the finest shots in that region.

This memorial marker identifies the cemetery where Collier is buried in Greenville, Mississippi.

Defeated Union soldiers fall back to the Potomac River, carrying their fallen leader, Colonel Edward Baker.

Union Colonel Edward Baker, also a U.S. senator, was shot dead by a Rebel sharpshooter at the Battle of Ball's Bluff.

shooters not to shoot Union soldiers on outpost duty? And did he think men willing to shoot pickets would not shoot generals? Even after the major bloodletting at Bull Run, *Harper's Weekly* noted, "Picket-firing is not considered humane business in modern warfare."

A proper respect for the very real threat of well-placed Rebel Minie balls had yet to take hold. On 21 October 1861, a lifelong friend of Abraham Lincoln's, Colonel Edward Baker—after whom the president named his second son—led a brigade-sized diversionary attack across the Potomac, 30 miles northwest of Washington. A Mexican War veteran, Baker was also a U.S. Senator from Oregon when he urged his men onward at the Battle of Ball's Bluff, making himself "a fair mark by his erect form and venerable appearance for the enemy's sharpshooters, of which numbers had climbed to the tree-tops

A Union picket collapses, shot by a hidden Confederate sharpshooter. Union General George McClellan thought sharpshooting "a barbarous practice."

A Sharpshooter General

No Civil War general so well appreciated and so wisely employed sharpshooters as CSA Major General Patrick Cleburne. From the Battle of Shiloh—where he hastily assembled volunteer marksmen to support Brigadier General Benjamin Prentiss in the Hornets' Nest—to all his future engagements, Cleburne believed in the wise application of precision rifle fire.

An Irishman by birth, he had served three years in the Royal Army's 41st Foot before immigrating to America. Practicing law in Arkansas, he joined the Confederate cause and soon was respected as an inspiring leader and talented tactician, nicknamed the "Stonewall Jackson of the West."

With the encouragement of their division commander, Cleburne's sharpshooters acquired more long-range rifles than any other division—some 26 Whitworths and 10 Kerrs—and put them to good use. A product of the British training system, Cleburne insisted on excellent instruction and constant drills. One sharpshooter recalled:

> "The men were drilled in camp, on the march, and even on the field of battle in judging distances. They would be halted, for instance, and required to guess at the distance of a certain point ahead and then measure by steps on their way. When firing, these men were never in haste; the distance of a line of men, of a horse, and artillery ammunition chest, was carefully decided upon; the telescope adjusted along its arc to give the proper elevation; the gun rested against a tree, across a log or in the fork of the rest stick [tripod] carried for that purpose."

Major General Patrick Cleburne, "Stonewall Jackson of the West," was a shrewd employer of sharpshooters.

Led by Lieutenant Abraham "Buck" Schell, this tiny band of superb marksmen included up to 30 men, among them Stan C. Harley, Walter L. Bragg, James Griswold, Charles Trickett, Walter Norris, John C. Knox, James Lane, Sam Mizer, John (or George) Decker, John McKinney, John Driscoll, Barney Roark, James Patterson, and Lieurgus A. Saller.

Cleburne was so interested in his divisional sharpshooters that they reported to him or his staff directly for daily instructions and were shrewdly employed to exploit their capabilities to the max. For example, on 26 July 1863, "I had no ammunition to spare," he wrote to his Corps commander, Lieutenant General William Hardee. Therefore, to keep pressure on the enemy while conserving ammunition, he employed five Whitworth sharpshooters, "which appeared to do good service. Mounted men were struck at distances ranging from 700 to 1300 yards."

Never shy about his deepest beliefs, Cleburne pointedly insisted that he never had and never would own slaves, and raised Southern eyebrows in 1864 when he advocated emancipating African Americans who were willing to join the Confederate cause. It was too late, however, for both Patrick Cleburne and his cause—he was killed on 30 November 1864 while leading an assault at Franklin, Tennessee.

General Cleburne's division had more Whitworth- and Kerr-armed sharpshooters than any other Confederate division.

Quite likely the only monument to an individual Confederate sharpshooter, this towering figure of Georgia marksman Berry Benson overlooks downtown Augusta, Georgia. Below are Generals Robert E. Lee, Thomas R.R. Cobb, William Henry Walker, and Andrew Jackson.

Brigadier General Ben McCulloch, CSA.

from the first and kept up a constant fire, especially singling out officers whenever they appeared." When sharpshooter fire unmanned an artillery piece, Colonel Baker grabbed several men and put it back into action—and instantly fell, shot dead by a sharpshooter. Dragging along their leader's body, Baker's demoralized troops retreated to the Potomac in terrible disorder, with many men shot and swept away in its turgid waters.

In the West, too, senior commanders did not fare well when they ignored the dangers of Confederate sharpshooters. At the Battle of Wilson's Creek, Missouri, on 10 August 1861, General Nathaniel Lyon rode his horse among advancing Union infantrymen, swinging his hat aloft and waving them forward. Wounded slightly, Lyon was unhorsed and stunned. Atop a second mount, he continued shouting and waving his hat—and this time the Missouri sharpshooter's round impacted center-chest. Not only did Lyon die, but his leaderless army lost the field and the battle.

The victor that day at Wilson's Creek, Brigadier General Ben McCulloch, a veteran of the Texas War of Independence and prominent member of his state's legislature, would have stood well to have learned from the death of Lyon. In fact, quite the opposite occurred, for on 7 March 1862 at the Battle of Elkhorn Tavern, General McCulloch's "dress attracted attention," one account discloses. "He wore a dress of black velvet, patent-leather high-top boots, and he had on a light-colored broad-brimmed Texan hat." One well-aimed Union bullet snuffed his life as surely as his opponent Lyon's had been snuffed months earlier.

CONFEDERATE SHARPSHOOTERS REORGANIZED

More than half the Civil War had passed before sharpshooting became an object of significant interest to the Confederate Army's leadership, which until then had left such issues to individual brigade and regimental commanders. Following the setbacks of 1863—Gettysburg in the east and Vicksburg in the west—and their army's declining strength, the importance of sharpshooting came to the fore. In modern terms, the sharpshooters' potential as a "force multiplier"—inflicting considerable damage on the enemy at a proportionally small investment—received proper regard.

Early in 1864, General Robert E. Lee directed the 36 infantry brigades in his Army of Northern Virginia to organize formal sharpshooter battalions, drawing together each regiment's finest rifle shots. This worked out to one company of sharpshooters, about 50 men, per regiment, with usually a five-company battalion per brigade. This did not always prove to be the case. The 13th Virginia Infantry Regiment could muster only about 20 picked men as sharpshooters, while reflecting a larger brigade of seven regiments, Major William Dunlop's South Carolina sharpshooter battalion had almost 250 marksmen. In the case of Captain Robert F. Ward's sharpshooters, drawn from the 42nd Mississippi Infantry Regiment, this meant simply "one sharpshooter for every ten men present for duty."

Above: Confederate sharpshooters pick off Union soldiers manning a defensive work, 1862.

Right: Confederate Major William S. Dunlop commanded a South Carolina sharpshooter battalion.

The Smartest Commander

The most adept commander I've come upon for countering Civil War sharpshooters is Colonel Robert C. Newton of the 5th Arkansas Cavalry. His sophisticated, flexible tactics worked superbly, marking him as a master tactician and his techniques worthy of elaboration. On 4 December 1863, he reported his engagement at Pine Bluff, Arkansas, which included the following details:

> "The enemy's sharpshooters now commenced firing upon me from the different houses along the lower edge of town, and, ordering Pratt to turn his fire upon them, I advanced Wood's and Chenoweth's skirmishers, and soon drove the Federal sharpshooters out of the houses in which they had first concealed themselves. They fell back to the houses on the next street, and, being strengthened from toward the court house, they kept up a brisk fire upon me. Finding that they would have me at a disadvantage should I waste time in sharpshooting with them, I pushed forward my skirmishers and charged with Wood's and Chenoweth's commands, driving the enemy through the houses, and inclosures in the town, until I reached the block upon which the residence of Anthony Rodgers stands, where I halted to give the men breathing time and to reform my line. . . . I concluded, inasmuch as the firing had ceased . . . to push my sharpshooters up as close to the enemy as could be done without too much exposure, and not charge, if at all, until I could rely upon being supported by at least Greene's column. . . . Brisk skirmishing continued all the time between my sharpshooters and those of the enemy. I ordered up Pratt's battery, and put it in position at the southwest corner of Rodger's inclosure, and opened with it upon the courthouse and the adjoining buildings, in which the enemy's sharpshooters were posted. In a short time he had silenced such of them as were firing from the cupola of the courthouse and those in Rodgers' storehouse. . . ."

Applying relentless pressure, flexibly employing skirmishers, then sharpshooters, and finally artillery, Colonel Newton had contained, compressed, and finally destroyed the enemy sharpshooters with minimal losses to his own forces.

Despite such differences, for the first time there was a degree of uniformity in Southern sharpshooter units, with command-level emphasis on selecting the best soldiers and properly training them so they'd be ready for the spring 1864 campaign. Major Dunlop, author of an excellent postwar history (*Lee's Sharpshooters*), detailed his men's range estimation training:

> "A man or an object the size of a man was stationed in front at an unknown distance, about 100 yards off; at the call of each name, the man stepped forward ten paces, surveyed carefully the object in front, calculated the intervening space, and deliberately announced in exact figures his estimate of the distance . . . then the next in the same way, and so on through the entire command. The distance was increased from one hundred to two, three, five and nine hundred yards, and an accurate account kept of each man's judgment in each drill . . . until each man could tell, almost to a mathematical certainty, the distance from any given point . . ."

Those who could not master range estimation were returned to their units.

Equally demanding was marksmanship training. Beginning at 100 yards and firing into a 5-

inch bull's-eye, the sharpshooters shot at progressively greater distances until, at 900 yards, the target was 6 x 6 feet with a 45-inch bull's-eye. Despite the South's persistent shortage of powder and projectiles, the sharpshooters fired untold amounts of ammunition. "A thousand or more of them were banging away for hours," wrote sharpshooter battalion commander Major Eugene Blackford, "until my head would ache from the noise and the smell of the saltpeter." Georgia sharpshooter Berry Benson noted that this practice firing integrated range estimation, "for it is essential to a soldier to know how far his enemy is from him in order to adjust his sights properly."

With practice Dunlop's men became so proficient, he wrote, that "the results achieved in estimating distance and rifle training were as amazing to the brigade commander as they were gratifying to the officers and men of the battalion."

Trained and ready for combat, the South's newly organized sharpshooter battalions would strike a mighty toll starting that spring of 1864.

CHAPTER TWO

Sharpshooters of the Union

In the war's earliest days, a disparity already was realized in the North. "However imperfect and crude their equipment and materiel," observed a Union officer, "man for man, [Southerners] were the superiors of their northern antagonists in the use of arms. . . . Indeed, there were in many regiments in the northern armies men who had never even fired a gun" prior to enlistment.

While this was entirely correct, an accomplished New York businessman equally realized that throughout the North were thousands of men like himself, who shot rifles competitively

Colonel Hiram Berdan, the Army of the Potomac's Chief of Sharpshooters, and the popular sharpshooter "California Joe." (Courtesy of the Vermont Historical Society.)

The front page of *Harper's Weekly,* 5 October 1861, depicts Berdan's Sharpshooters training at Weehawen, New Jersey.

RECRUITS WANTED
FOR THE
1st REGIMENT OF U. S. SHARP-SHOOTERS!

The undersigned will be at _____

On _____ 1862,
for the purpose of enlisting men for the **First Regiment of United**
States Sharp-Shooters, now at Washington. None but good ablebodied men will be received.
The Regiment is to be armed with Sharpe's improved Target
Rifles, which are to be furnished the Regiment by the 20th inst.

Headquarters at the City of Lansing, two doors below Bailey's Bank, on Michigan Avenue.

Recruits will be received for about THIRTY DAYS only.

Lansing, February 10th, 1862.

J. H. BAKER,
1st Lieut. Co. C., 1st Regt. U.S.S.S.

All across the North in 1861, the call went out for sharp-shooters. Even German-American marksmen were urged to try out for Indiana's Turner Sharpshooter Company (right).

Riflemen,
ATTENTION !

A COMPANY OF ONE HUNDRED MEN to be selected from the
BEST RIFLE SHOTS,
In the State, is to be raised to act as a **COMPANY OF SHARP SHOOTERS** through the War. Each man will be entitled to
A BOUNTY OF $22,00,
When mustered into the service of the United States, and
100,00 DOLLARS
at the close of the War, in addition to his regular pay.

No man will be accepted or mustered into service who is not an active and able bodied man, and who cannot when firing at a rest at a distance of two hundred yards, put ten consecutive shots into a target the average distance not to exceed five inches from the centre of the bull's eye to the centre of the ball; and all candidates will have to pass such an examination as to satisfy the recruiting officer of their fitness for enlistment in this corps.

Recruits having Rifles to which they are accustomed are requested to bring them to the place of rendezvous.

Recruits will be received by **JAMES D. FESSENDEN,**
Adams Block, No. 23, Market Square, PORTLAND, Maine.

Sept. 16, 1861.

1ST REGIMENT

BERDAN'S U. S.

SHARPSHOOTERS !

Lieut. Winthrop, detailed from Washington to recruit for this Regiment will
"SHOOT IN"
all who may apply, this day, in the field in rear of residence of S. Arnold Esq.

Shooting to commence at 8 o'clock, A. M. and at 2 o'clock, P. M.
Saturday, 26, Oct., 1861.

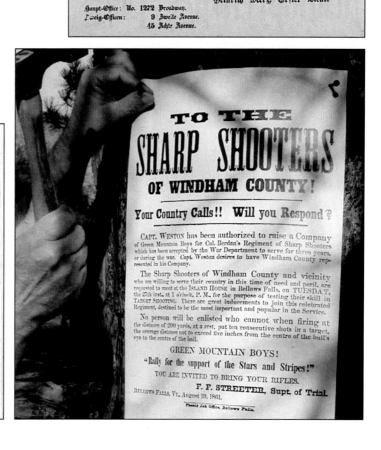

and could match or even outshoot the Confederacy's finest riflemen. Hiram Berdan was so certain of it that he contacted President Abraham Lincoln directly and offered to raise an entire regiment of such advanced marksmen. After the poor showing of Union forces in the war's initial clashes, Berdan traveled to Washington in June 1861 and soon obtained endorsements from President Lincoln and Secretary of War Simon Cameron. Thus, on 15 June 1861, the Union Army's commanding general authorized the newly appointed Colonel Hiram Berdan to raise the 1st U.S. Sharpshooter Regiment.

In the tradition of Revolutionary War sharpshooters, Berdan's recruits were invited to bring along their own target-grade rifles, for which the federal government would reimburse them—and they'd certainly need them. Unlike many alleged "sharpshooters," these candidates had to pass a challenging marksmanship test to join the 1st Sharpshooter Regiment. All across the North—New York, Michigan, New Hampshire, Vermont, Wisconsin, Maine, Minnesota, and Pennsylvania—state governors agreed to contribute companies of sharpshooters. Bold posters announced local shooting tryouts, and soon the Union's best rifle shots were firing Berdan's test, which required "a string of 10 shots at a distance of 200 yards, the aggregate measurement of which should not exceed 50 inches." In other words, the rifleman had to place each shot within 5 inches of the target's dead center. This was no simple feat.

Vermont rifleman Charles Fairbanks well expressed the pressure he felt:

> "It was with fear and almost trembling that I took the rifle in hand to determine whether or not I was fit for a sharpshooter. There was a large crowd of townspeople present, who seemed to be about evenly divided in my favor of my going to war, but after making the first shot at the ten-inch ring target, there was a cheer from the spectators, for I had put a bullet nearly in the center of the bulls eye, which was about two inches in diameter. The remaining nine shots were put inside the ring about as per sketch with a cheer from the crowd after each shot."

Reflecting the patriotic sentiment of the times, so many fine riflemen like Fairbanks came forward and passed Berdan's test that he obtained authority to raise a second unit, the 2nd U.S. Sharpshooter Regiment.

PREPARING FOR WAR

Soon after Berdan's volunteers assembled and began training near Washington, the impracticality of lugging into combat 30-pound, heavy-barreled rifles with delicate scopes became apparent. The

Berdan the Sharpshooter

Flamboyant, proud, urbane, and technologically brilliant, Hiram Berdan was the driving force that founded the Union Army's sharpshooter regiments. A man of considerable wealth yielded by a variety of mechanical inventions, Berdan had been a competitive rifleman since the early 1850s. Favoring heavy-barreled match rifles with scopes or precise globe sights, he soon earned fame as the nation's top rifle shot.

This combination of wealth and prestige gained Berdan the connections to go directly to President Abraham Lincoln and urge creation of a sharpshooting unit. His personal shooting abilities, documented in several accounts, were nothing short of superb. In October 1861, while President Lincoln and General George McClellan watched, Berdan fired a string of shots at 600 yards, all of which hit the head of a Jefferson Davis effigy target. One shot, which he called when taunted by Assistant Secretary of War Thomas Scott, unerringly struck the target's right eye, evoking laughter from President Lincoln.

Although wearing a colonel's uniform and, as the Army of the Potomac's Chief of Sharpshooters, commanding two sharpshooter regiments, underneath it all Berdan remained a civilian lacking in military training and experience. Fortunately, most often he deferred tactical decisions to his qualified subordinates and occupied him-

Colonel Hiram Berdan, founder of the Union Army's sharpshooter regiments.

self in a military version of "office politics," at which he was fairly adept. Despite criticisms and backbiting from a variety of officers, he left active duty in 1864 with his reputation intact and focused on an assortment of military inventions, including the metallic cartridge primer that bears his name to this day.

Colonel Berdan fires a long-range demonstration early in 1861.

sharpshooter regiments needed a more-rugged, more easily wielded weapon. Always an advocate of emerging technology, Colonel Berdan initially believed that a repeating rifle was ideal—especially in the hands of superb marksmen, who could make each shot count. Thus, their heavy "telescope" rifles were collected and stored in the wagons that followed the units, available when needed, while day-

A squad from the 2nd U.S. Sharpshooter Regiment with Colt rifles. They are (left to right): Private Charles Applin, Private Isaac Farnum, Sergeant Horace Caldwell, Private Amos Abbott, Private William Beard, Private William Spead, and Private Cyrus Farnum.

to-day armament became a five-shot, .56-caliber Colt revolving rifle. Although not a tack-driver, a repeating rifle in 1861 posed a significant advantage over single-shot Confederate rifles.

Next, Berdan obtained for his men uniforms that were identical to other Union soldiers' blue garb except for the color—*green*. Not only was this a sharpshooter's symbol of pride and a continuation of the rifleman's green hunting shirts under George Washington, but it was also a useful form of camouflage that undoubtedly saved many sharpshooters' lives.

A *New York Post* article described how Berdan's men were to be employed:

> "The Corps of Sharpshooters will be used not in the midst of battle, but on the outskirts, where, beyond the smoke and fury of the engagement, they will act independently, choose their objects and make every shot tell. Posted in small squads at from one-eighth to three-eighths of a mile from the field, firing a shot a minute, and hitting their mark with almost a dead certainty, they will be a great annoyance to the enemy. They will combine their attention to the officers, and by picking these off, will bring confusion into the enemy's lines."

This was not entirely correct, but it captured the flavor of what Berdan intended to achieve: "to hit a man every time at one-eighth of a mile, hit him two out of three times at a quarter-mile, and three out of five times at a half-mile." While this was technologically feasible, it would prove an antiseptic (and naïve) view of the bitter, bloody battles to come. As one recruit wrote after the war, Colonel Berdan "made it appear that all we would have to do would be to pick off Rebel officers and other troublesome Rebels."

In addition to Berdan's 1st and 2nd U.S. Sharpshooter Regiments, other genuine sharpshooter

California Joe

In a unit composed of many distinct characters, a Berdan Sharpshooter really had to stand out to be a prominent personality. Such was the 1st Regiment's Company C's Truman Head, popularly known as "California Joe" or simply "Californey."

One of Berdan's oldest men at age 52, California Joe was soft spoken, with "an eye as keen as a hawk." A fellow sharpshooter called him "one of the mildest [and] gentlest of men" and "entirely free from brag and bluster." From his days in the California mountains, he sported "an endowment of hair and whiskers Reuben would have liked for a patriarchal portrait."

Born in Otsego, New York, Head got his nickname from being a forty-niner gold prospector. He listed his occupation as "hunter," referring to his success at bagging grizzly bears.

Head carried his own privately purchased Sharps target rifle, the only one in the regiment until June 1862, when the entire unit received Sharps rifles. Quite likely it was Head who persuaded Colonel Berdan that this was the regiment's ideal weapon. Often, though, he fired a heavy-barreled target rifle when shooting beyond 500 yards.

"His unerring rifle has made many a rebel bite the dust," observed *Harper's*.

For instance, when a Rebel sharpshooter firing from inside a brick chimney at 500 yards shot several Union soldiers, California Joe was called in. He arrived with an octagon-barreled target rifle with a telescopic sight. His first three shots chipped off pieces of brick around the narrow firing port, but the fourth round connected. When later that position was captured, it was found the Rebel sharpshooter "had been shot between the eyes."

Again it was a heavy, 32-pound target rifle that he used in another recorded encounter, this time against a Confederate artillery position. Seeing his crews hesitating to man the guns, a Rebel officer jumped atop the parapet and waved his sword to come forward and load. That's where Californey's shot caught him, sending the artillerymen scrambling back to cover. "It was a fine shot," said a witness, "for the man must have been a full half-mile away," or about 800 yards.

California Joe dodged more than a few bullets himself, his closest call coming at Malvern Hill, Virginia, in July 1862, when a Rebel sharpshooter's bullet hit his Sharps rifle's band and fragmented into pieces that wounded his nose and cheek. Though he fully recovered, by the fall of 1862 California Joe's age caught up with him. His eyes failing him, he came down with jaundice and was hospitalized. Afterward he was discharged due to a permanent disability.

He returned to California and spent the rest of his days as a U.S. Customs Inspector in San Francisco. When he passed away in 1888, a monument was erected to him there.

"Watchin' for a Reb." Berdan Sharpshooter Truman "California Joe" Head demonstrates hiding from enemy observation. *(Courtesy of the Vermont Historical Society.)*

Distinctive Insignia

Members of the 1st and 2nd U.S. Sharpshooter Regiments wore distinctive green uniforms, the only Union force so attired and a source of considerable pride. Additionally, their officers' hats bore badges with the unit's emblazoned silver initials, USSS, for United States Sharp Shooters.

A few other (extremely rare) Civil War sharpshooter insignias exist. When New York's 56th Volunteer Infantry Regiment mustered in 1861, its organization included one sharpshooter element from Sullivan County, designated as Company L. "The members were selected for their superior marksmanship," a regimental history notes, "all being experienced hunters and woodsmen and experts with the rifle." Early in the war, these prized marksmen

Officers of the 1st and 2nd U.S. Sharpshooter Regiments wore this unique hat badge.

wore a 6-inch green felt shield on their right breast, with an "X" in the center.

At least one Confederate sharpshooter unit also wore unique insignia. According to Joe Long, Curator of History at South Carolina's Confederate Relic Room and Museum, Sergeant W.T. McGill of Dunlop's Sharpshooter Battalion reported his unit's sharpshooters "were distinguished by a badge consisting of a red band running diagonally across the left elbow of the coat sleeve with a red star just above the band." Not only did this identify the soldier as an outstanding marksman, but that insignia "would pass [allow] the Sharp Shooter anywhere." Thus, he could roam his regiment's lines and forward positions in search of shooting opportunities.

units were organized. For example, two companies of Massachusetts men had passed Berdan's test but instead became the 1st and 2nd Companies of Massachusetts Sharpshooters, or "Andrews Sharpshooters," after their governor. Indiana's 32nd Infantry Regiment recruited a company of German-born marksmen, *Die Turner Schutzenkompanie* (Turner's Sharpshooter Company), which proved worthy of the title. Ohio raised 10 independent sharpshooter companies during the war. And farther west, Colonel John W. Birge raised a regiment that would earn renown as "Birge's Western Sharpshooters" (see "Birge's Western Sharpshooters," page 30). And, of course, there were others.

U.S. SHARPSHOOTER REGIMENTS' FIRST BLOOD

Having trained through the winter of 1861–62, by spring Berdan's Sharpshooter Regiments were ready for action. Accompanying General George McClellan's Army of the Potomac, they landed on Chesapeake Bay, 60 miles southeast of Richmond, to bypass the extensive works defending northeast Virginia. When McClellan besieged the Rebel's coastal fortifications at Yorktown, Berdan's men experienced their first taste of battle, especially focusing their fire on enemy artillery positions.

"Gun after gun was silenced and abandoned," recorded a sharpshooter officer, "until within an hour every embrasure within a range of a thousand yards to the right and left was tenantless and silent." Return fire did little to stop the sharpshooters. "Their infantry," the officer continued, "which at first responded with a vigorous fire, found that exposure of a head meant grave danger if not death."

Unaccustomed to such concentrated, well-aimed fire, Confederate troops beyond the front lines moved about openly—but not for long. While an officer observed through binoculars, "a few shots were fired by picked men . . . to ascertain the exact range, which was then announced and the order given, 'Commence firing.'" The result was deadly, and the Rebels quickly learned to avoid unnecessary exposure at any distance.

Confederate sharpshooters firing from concealed rifle pits proved their most difficult foes, keeping up "an annoying fire from which the Union artillerists suffered severely." Because these shooters were "usually behind a cover of nature or artificially planted bushes . . . it was almost impossible to dislodge their occupants; every puff of smoke from one of them was, of course, the signal for a heavy fire of Union rifles." But the savvy Rebel shooters would duck below ground, wait for attention to shift elsewhere, and then plink away again.

One "particularly obnoxious and skillful rifleman" at Yorktown engaged a Berdan Sharpshooter in a classic sniper duel, one of the earliest ever recorded. Private John S.M. Ide, a New Hampshire man with the 1st Regiment's Company E, "devoted himself" to finding and eliminating the troublesome Confederate marksman. As he fired a heavy target rifle with telescopic sight, Ide's exchange "was watched with the keenest interest by those not otherwise engaged." Several shots went back and forth, "but fortune first smiled on the rebel, and Ide fell dead, shot through the forehead while in the act of raising his rifle to aim." Ide was the regiment's first man killed in action. The duel, however, was not over.

Lieutenant Colonel William Y.W. Ripley, the 1st Regiment's executive officer and himself an excellent shot, saw Ide fall. Earning "the admiration of hundreds of eye witnesses," Lieutenant Colonel Ripley strolled over "while bullets plowed and dusted the ground around him," picked up the fallen man's loaded rifle, and announced, "I'll try him a shot at one notch

Sergeant James W. Staples, 1st U.S. Sharpshooter Regiment, with a Colt revolving, five-shot repeater. Staples was killed on 30 June 1862 at the Battle of New Market, Virginia.

Birge's Western Sharpshooters

In the Civil War's opening year, a counterpart to Berdan's Sharpshooters was organized in the Union Army's Western Department, known as "Birge's Western Sharpshooters." Commanded by Colonel John W. Birge, it was the brainchild of Major General John C. Freemont, one of Lincoln's original four senior commanders. Freemont wanted Birge's Sharpshooters to be elite marksmen and serve as his scouts and skirmishers. Three companies were recruited from Ohio and three from Illinois, while individual recruits from Iowa, Wisconsin, Michigan, and Minnesota fleshed out three more companies.

Their unique armament was the Dimick American Deer and Target Rifle, a heavy-barreled percussion firearm manufactured in St. Louis, Missouri. General Freemont even designed a distinctive headgear for them, which incorporated three squirrel tails, giving them the nickname "The Squirrel Tails."

General Fremont's replacement, Major General Henry Halleck, wisely employed Birge's men, inflicting a lopsided 4:1 casualty rate at the Battle of Mt. Zion, which Halleck thought "resulted from the long range rifles of our sharpshooters." When attached to Brigadier General Ben Prentiss' brigade at Fort Donelson, however, a sharpshooter recorded, "Here the general was a little perplexed to know what to do with Deer rifles without bayonets and did a terrible amount of swearing because the Regiment was armed with that type of rifle; but, finally concluded to let them fight in their own way."

Fighting in their own way deeply impressed General Lew Wallace, who watched as "they dispersed, and, like Indians, sought cover to please themselves behind rocks and stumps, or in hollows. Sometimes they dug holes; sometimes they climbed into trees. Once in a good location they remained there all day. At night they would crawl out and report in camp."

At the Battle of Fort Donelson, *Harper's Weekly* noted that these "keen-eyed" sharpshooters, firing from 300 yards, engaged any Confederate head to show above the works. "The fire was so incessant and so fatal," it noted, "that the Confederates were allowed no rest except in their uncomfortable rifle ditches, it being impossible to reach their tents over the ridge without exposure." Colonel Jacob G. Lauman verifies this, writing that Colonel Birge's Sharpshooter Regiment "deserves great credit for its part in the capture of Fort Donelson," in particular for their precision shooting, "which told severely on the Confederate gunners serving the battery." This fire, the unit history notes, "made it possible for General C.F. Smith to gain the heights and for General Grant to capture Fort Donelson . . . the following day." This was Grant's first major victory.

Company C, "Birge's Western Sharpshooters" or the 66th Illinois Infantry Regiment, at Camp Davies, Mississippi, 1863. Armed here with Dimick Deer and Target Rifles, the sharpshooters soon acquired Henry lever-action rifles. (Photo © Bureau County Historical Society, Princeton, IL 61356.)

Afterward the sharpshooters fought at Shiloh; then, disregarding the men's diverse origins, the regiment was renamed the 14th Missouri Infantry Volunteers and assigned a new commander. At the Battle of Corinth, Mississippi, their exacting fire helped turn back a major Confederate assault. One Rebel leader, Colonel William P. Rogers, commanding the 2nd Texas Infantry, was slain by concentrated sharpshooter fire, his body struck no fewer than 11 times.

Now suffering under commanders who didn't realize their capabilities, the sharpshooters spent months on rear-echelon details in Corinth. Then in November 1862, the regiment was redesignated the 66th Illinois Infantry, a title it would carry to the end of the war. Another year of misemployment followed, with the unit operating a POW stockade and securing rear areas from "rebel scouts and guerrillas."

Frustrated by their Dimick rifles' low rate of fire, that fall of 1863 every man in the regiment anted up $43 (three months' pay) to privately purchase Henry repeaters, the world's first reliable lever-action rifle. "This arm did much to make the Regiment famous," the unit history notes, "and the men who purchased them with their own means deserve credit." What they had given up in maximum range, they believed, was more than made up in sheer firepower, an unbelievable 17 rounds! The Union Army refused to reimburse them for the rifles but agreed to provide ammunition. Outside Atlanta, Private Prosper Bowe recalled how well the Henrys worked:

"[W]hen the order was given to open on them we started our seventeen shooters to work. The first column in front of us nearly all fell at the first two volleys but they stood their ground well. . . . I stood and fired ninety rounds without stopping. My gun barrel was so hot that I could not touch it. Spit on it and it would siz . . ."

At Rome Crossroads on 16 May 1864, the sharpshooters suffered considerable casualties, including their regimental commander, Colonel Patrick Burke, who died of his wounds. Attributing the heavy losses to the "foolhardiness" of a Captain Taylor, unit historian Lorenzo Barker noted that before the action Taylor had declared, "I will either have a larger stripe [promotion] on my shoulders or I will leave my body on the field." Barker recalls, "He left his body on the field, he was shot square through the forehead."

The 66th Illinois fought in the Atlanta Campaign and then in Sherman's March to the Sea, demonstrating great shooting skill and an incredible rate of fire. By the end of hostilities, some 244 sharpshooters had been killed or wounded.

higher anyway." Cranking up the telescope, Ripley took careful aim when "the triumphant rebel, made bold by his success, raised himself into view." Firing at almost the same instant, the Rebel sharpshooter's shot splattered harmlessly behind Ripley, but most believed the colonel had felled his man, for no further shots followed.

On 4 May the Confederates abandoned Yorktown, falling back toward Richmond. In this, Berdan's Sharpshooters' first battle, the *New York Herald* declared that their "unerring accuracy of shots at long range has caused a universality of bewilderment." General Fitz-John Porter, whose division they'd supported, congratulated their "good service in picking off the enemy's skirmishers and artillerists whenever they should show themselves."

The campaign continued, the Army of the Potomac again pushing toward Richmond. Soon, however, massing Confederate forces slowed the advance and then halted it entirely, and eventually General McClellan was obligated to turn back toward the coast, fighting a series of clashes called the Seven Days Campaign. On 1 July the Union Army went into defense at Malvern Hill, and here, again, Berdan's Sharpshooters demonstrated their remarkable abilities. While Union gunboats in the nearby James River threw covering fire over the sharpshooters' heads, they fought head-on against approaching Rebel forces.

A column of draft horses dragging artillery pieces galloped into an open field before them. "As the head of the column turned to the right to go into battery, every rifle within range was brought to bear, and horses and men began to fall rapidly," wrote an eyewitness. Ignoring the deadly fire, the artillerymen "pressed on, and when there were no longer horses to haul the guns, the gunners sought to put their pieces into battery by hand; nothing, however, could stand before that terrible storm of lead, and after ten minutes of gallant effort the few survivors, leaving their guns in the open field, took shelter in the friendly woods." The destroyed battery was McCarthy's Richmond Howitzers, manned by some of Virginia's most prominent sons, now mostly dead or wounded. For many it was their first fight—and their last. So deadly was the sharpshooter fire that "not a gun was afterward placed or fired from that quarter during the day." Describing that terrible action after the war, one battery survivor said, "We went in a battery and came out a wreck. We staid [sic] ten minutes . . . and came out with one gun, ten men and two horses without firing a shot."

The battle, however, was not one-sided. After the Confederate attackers had been beat back, the scale of this terrible bloodletting became clear. Some 16,000 Federal troops had been killed or wounded during the Seven Days Campaign, plus a staggering 20,600 Confederates. The Berdan Sharpshooters, who'd totally expended their ammunition, had suffered major casualties, too, with some companies having half their men killed or wounded. After Malvern Hill, it would take months to receive and train replacements.

Among the seriously wounded was Lieutenant Colonel Ripley, who at Yorktown had engaged the Rebel sharpshooter who killed Private Ide. Narrowly avoiding amputation of his right leg, Ripley's military service was over. But his gallantry at Yorktown and Malvern Hill, "above and beyond the call of duty," did not go unrecognized. He was awarded the Medal of Honor, the first U.S. sharpshooter so honored.

Noticing the dwindling sharpshooter ranks as they passed before him, General McClellan said, "It's too bad! But they are good what's left of them."

ATTITUDES ABOUT SHARPSHOOTERS

Depending on the source, Berdan's men and their Confederate counterparts were considered bloodthirsty assassins, unexcitable target shooters, elite warriors, undisciplined prima donnas—respected, detested—all these things and more.

Who Shot Ben McCulloch?

Sharpshooters who killed general officers in the Civil War mostly remain anonymous. In many cases sharpshooters were too preoccupied with the tactical situation and likely fired at too great a distance to notice more than that they'd unhorsed a man or that his location or actions had suggested the target was an officer. In many cases, sharpshooters fired so quickly against a variety of fleeting targets that there was no time to digest whom they had shot. And other sharpshooters, even if they knew, did not desire the "credit" for what many considered a grisly act of deliberate killing.

On the other hand, occasionally there were conflicting claims, such as in the case of Brigadier General Ben McCulloch. Several postwar books accredited that fatal shot to the legendary gunfighter, James "Wild Bill" Hickok, who indeed was present at Elkhorn Tavern as a Union scout and sharpshooter. Hickok's own biography, *Wild Bill*, asserts he spent that day "lying behind a large log on a hill overlooking Cross-Timber Hollow for nearly four hours, picking off Confederates. His victims numbered thirty-five, and were of all ranks, from the private soldier to Gen. McCulloch." Serious historians doubt Hickok's claim, pointing out that official records attribute the kill to an Illinois infantryman.

In fact, Union Colonel Nicholas Greusel, commanding the 2nd Brigade of the 1st Division at Elkhorn Tavern, officially reported, "It was during this skirmish that the officer supposed to be General Ben McCulloch was shot by Peter Pelican of Company B, Thirty-Sixth Illinois Volunteers." Greusel's report is considered the authoritative account.

Then was Wild Bill Hickok's claim an exaggeration or an outright lie? His other assertion—that he shot 35 Confederate soldiers that day—is certainly hard to believe . . . unless you know a bit more about Wild Bill.

Union scout-sharpshooter James "Wild Bill" Hickok, later a legendary Western gunfighter.

After the Civil War, Wild Bill became a famous Western gunfighter, and his handiness with a gun or his readiness to use it in a life-and-death fight is no myth. For some 26 years as a lawman and as a private citizen, Hickok fought and won well-documented gunfights in Kansas, Nebraska, Colorado, Missouri, and South Dakota. At a distance of 75 yards— with a revolver—he shot dead Dave Tutt in Springfield, Missouri, "with a shot squarely into Tutt's chest." Possessing legendary shooting skills matched by an equally grim attitude, when firing from a tactically advantageous position Hickok certainly could have gunned down 35 Confederate soldiers on 7 March 1862.

What then about the claim that he shot General McCulloch? In fact, it's entirely possible that both Peter Pelican and Wild Bill shot Confederate generals that day. For, no sooner had McCulloch fallen than Brigadier General James M. McIntosh was killed "while leading a charge to recover McCulloch's body." Yes, *two generals* fell at Elkhorn Tavern, nearly side by side, to such catastrophic effect that Confederate forces lost the day and, with it, control of the state of Arkansas to Union forces.

After Wild Bill was murdered in Deadwood, South Dakota, he was properly interred like the great marksman that he was. "We buried him in a rough coffin with his big Sharps rifle by his side," reported a friend. "His left arm was laid cross-wise, beneath his back, just as he carried it in life. His right arm was extended downward by his side with his hand resting on his rifle."

Native American Sharpshooters

In the summer of 1863, some 142 Chippewa, Menominee, and Huron Oneida Indians were recruited in Michigan and organized as Company K of the 1st Michigan Sharpshooter Regiment. The company's two most senior officers were white, but the other officer, Lieutenant Garrett A. Graveraet, was a Native American. The unit's roster lists many traditional family names, such as Mash-Kaw and Ne-so-Got and Pa-Ke-Mabo-Ga. Quite a few did not even speak English—not a problem since Lieutenant Graveraet and his Native American sergeants were bilingual.

An idealist and well educated, at the war's commencement Graveraet was teaching school to Indian children at Little Traverse Bay. For leisure, this man of sophisticated interests painted portraitures and landscapes and was an accomplished musician.

Despite being economically deprived, these men did not enlist simply for cash bonuses. "We are descendents of braves," declared Chief Nock-ke-chick-faw-me to his young warriors in 1863, asking them to be "heroic and brave" and join the Union cause. "If the South conquers," he warned, "you will be slaves, dogs. There will be no protection for us; we shall be driven from our homes, our lands, and the graves of our friends."

Unlike many Union sharpshooters, Company K's men brought a natural aptitude to their duties. Dwelling in Michigan's northern forests as subsistence hunters, they were masters of tracking, shooting, stalking, and camouflage. Finding their Union blue uniforms too conspicuous, Company K's Indians would "find a dry spot of earth and roll in it until their uniform was the complete color of the ground before going out on the skirmish line." On rainy days each Indian smeared mud over his clothing until

Two Native Americans are sworn in as Michigan Sharpshooters, 1861. (Courtesy of Wisconsin Historical Society.)

it was "the color of the earth." The whites of the 1st Michigan learned to do likewise, the regimental adjutant, Major Edward Buckbee, noted, enabling the regiment to do "the closest skirmishing at the least cost of any Regiment in the division."

Sergeant Wyman White, a Berdan Sharpshooter, encountered a Michigan Indian sharpshooter in Virginia, where both were targeted to suppress a Confederate artillery position. Sizing up the terrain, White noticed that the half-grown cornfield before him—the stalks hardly 2 feet high—would not allow concealed movement. This was not so to his Indian companion, who advised, "Make self corn. Do as I do." Cutting off a dozen corn stalks, the Indian stuffed them into his clothes and equipment. White did likewise, and both men crawled through the field without detection. Gaining a concealed spot, they shot away and "kept them from using the guns all afternoon." White never saw his stoic companion again.

The Confederates, too, found curious their encounters with these Michigan Indian sharpshooters. Major W.A. Smith of the 14th North Carolina Infantry recalled a clash in thick woods when his men believed the Indians, their backs against open fields, would be compelled to surrender or die. "When driven into the open they did not fire again at us, but ran like deer," he reported with surprise. "We captured not one of them."

Their shooting could be as effective as their stalking skills. At Cold Harbor, Company K's Indians focused their fire on the enemy's withdrawing artillery, disrupting every attempt to hitch horses to the guns. Their aim was sure, for afterward, another Union unit "found 26 dead horses at one battery, and 37 at another."

Wounded Native American sharpshooters, most likely of Company K, 1st Michigan Sharpshooter Regiment, during the Wilderness Campaign, 1864. (Courtesy of Library of Congress.)

Delaware Indian scouts between missions in a Union Army camp.

These Indians' warrior ethics at times had to be an inspiration to the men about them. For instance, the desertion of a young Chippewa soldier had a most remarkable result. When word reached his family back in Michigan, the deserter's middle-aged father, Ash-ka-buga-ma-ka, arrived unannounced at the company's field position in Virginia, having paid his own railway fare to get there. He enlisted in Company K, he explained, "to maintain the family's honor." He served honorably to the end of the war.

Some Company K sharpshooters were especially noteworthy, among them an elderly Chippewa marksman known as "Old One Eye." Somehow managing to get past recruiters with just one eye, according to a 1st Michigan officer, the old man "could see further and shoot quicker and more accurately with his left eye than most men could if they had a dozen eyes."

When a distant Rebel sharpshooter annoyed Brigadier General Orlando Wilcox's staff with a series of near-misses at Cold Harbor, One Eye was called in to hunt him down. Once briefed, the stoic old brave sat on the ground, just eyeing the headquarters area and surrounding woods, thinking, saying nothing for 30 minutes. Then he walked off. The following afternoon, a Union patrol reported a shot fired quite a ways off—not by the Rebel sharpshooter, but by some hidden rifleman who had shot the Rebel out of a tree. Old One Eye, when asked by the regimental adjutant what had happened, replied simply, "Me got 'im."

Another Indian sharpshooter, Antoine Scott, was cited in the Michigan Adjutant General's records for his valor at the Battle of the Crater: "Before Petersburg, July 30, 1864, instead of screening himself before the captured works, this soldier stood boldly up and deliberately fired his piece until the enemy was close upon him, when, instead of surrendering, he ran the gauntlet of shot and shell and escaped."

A third extraordinary sharpshooter was Private Daniel Mwa-ke-we-naw, 41, a powerful man who stood over 6 feet. At Spotsylvania, this superb rifleman was credited with shooting "not less than thirty-two rebels, a number of them officers." Wounded in the face, head, and hand, Mwa-ke-we-naw continued firing until he simply could not operate his rifle. His wounds were dressed, but he died of a resulting infection.

Spotsylvania also proved the darkest episode in Company K's history. Some 13 Native American sharpshooters died there, including Lieutenant Graveraet's father, a sergeant, killed instantly when a Minie ball struck him in the head. Hailing Company K's performance at Petersburg as "splendid work," a Union lieutenant also sadly reported, "Some of them were mortally wounded, and drawing up their blouses over their faces, they chanted a death song and died—four of them in a group."

Promoted and commanding the company at Petersburg, Lieutenant Graveraet, too, was severely wounded by an artillery shell. His left arm was amputated, but that did not save his life. On his deathbed, Graveraet insisted, "Fightin' for my Country is all right." He is buried on Mackinac Island, Michigan, beside his father. By the time they mustered out at the war's end, less than two-thirds of Company K's original enlistees were still alive.

Lieutenant Colonel Ripley of the 1st U.S. Sharpshooter Regiment observed:

> "Sharpshooting is the squirrel hunting of war; it is wonderful to see how self-forgetful the marksman grows—with sportsmanlike eyes he seeks out the grander game, and with coolness and accuracy he brings it down. At the moment he grows utterly indifferent to human life or human suffering, and seems intent only on cruelty and destruction; to make a good shot and hit his man, brings for the time being a feeling of immense satisfaction."

That description aptly fit many Confederates, too, who likened their role to one big hunting trip, such as Joseph Nesbett, an elder Tennessee sharpshooter. A companion reported, "Every time he shot he would blow the smoke out of his gun, as was his custom when squirrel shooting at home."

Others were antisocial firebrands. David "Old Dave" Temple of Andrews Sharpshooters, the best shot in his company, was a "reckless old Cuss and cares nothing for any body," wrote Private Roland Bowen. One day, he reported, "Old Dave" announced he'd "kill a few God damned Johnnys in revenge for the death of Capt. Saunders at Antietam." With two men, Temple slipped into a forward position "and proceeds to give them Hell. He bangs away all day." Both companions were seriously wounded, but "Old Dave" came back unscratched, happy that he had sent "20 damned Skunks of Hell to have a reckoning with their Eternal Creator."

For sheer audacity, it's difficult to exceed a gutsy Confederate sharpshooter who thought he was a one-man army, encountered at the Battle of the Wilderness by John Worsham, a Virginia soldier:

> "We found one Confederate soldier, an Alabaman, who was standing behind a large pine tree, loading and firing with as much deliberation as if he were firing at a target. He was keeping the whole of Hancock's force back at this point. He said he was a sharpshooter, and his line was on each side of him! There certainly was no other Confederate unit in front of our regiment line, nor could we see one either on the right or left."

Sharpshooters of both sides displayed an independent spirit that could verge on insubordination. Hungry, without rations for days, a body of Berdan's men marched along a Virginia road and called to passing officers, "Hardtack! Hardtack!" When Brigadier General John H. Ward and his staff rode past, again they hollered, "Hardtack!" Halting his horse and drawing a pistol, the arrogant Ward shouted, "God damn your souls to hell. The next man that says, 'Hardtack' I will put a ball through his head!" All was still. The general turned his horse and *every man in the regiment* yelled, "Hardtack!" Ward hesitated to make good his threat—all around he heard the "click" of cocking rifles—so off he rode. The only repercussion, one sharpshooter noted, was "the old puffball told the officers that he would hold them responsible for our good behavior, and that ended the matter."

The soldiers fired on by sharpshooters acquired a special loathing for these invisible killers who took lives detachedly at great range. "The dread of our sharpshooters is very great throughout the whole Rebel army," observed the *New York Herald* on 15 May 1862. Even Winslow Homer, the Civil War artist who drew a popular sketch of a Union sharpshooter in a tree, was no admirer. He confessed to a friend in 1862, "The above impression [a sketch of crosshairs over a human shape] struck me as being as near murder as anything I ever could think of in connection with the army, and I always had a horror of that branch of the service."

Harper's Weekly declared that sharpshooters "take the risk of being cut off by cavalry, or executed, as they certainly would be, if taken." Another observer thought them "not likely very often to be taken prisoners, as death is considered their just penalty; for as they very seldom are in a position to show mercy, so, in like manner, is mercy rarely shown them."

"What are we to do with these wretches?" asked the *Charleston Mercury* on 31 March 1862, referring to Berdan's Sharpshooters. "I answer, as Jackson did at Manassas when told that the enemy was driving us back. 'We give them the bayonet, sir—the bayonet!'"

"I hated sharpshooters," announced one Civil War veteran, "both Confederate and Union, and I was always glad to seen them killed." His was not a rare sentiment.

Nor was a sharpshooter's fear of capture unfounded. During the Peninsula Campaign, the *New York Herald* disclosed that when Private Joseph Durkee, a missing Berdan Sharpshooter, was found:

> "His head was riddled by a dozen bullets. The presumption is that he must have been shot after being killed, as a gratification to the fiendish hatred entertained toward our sharpshooters, who, through their watchful vigilance and unerring rifles, have worked such terrible destruction in their ranks."

A month later, soldiers of the 5th Wisconsin killed a Rebel soldier carrying Durkee's missing Colt rifle, returning it to Berdan's Sharpshooters.

Confederate sharpshooters, too, thought it hazardous to surrender to Union soldiers. At Gettysburg a captured Rebel marksman was certain he'd soon be shot—until, relieved, he learned his captors were his Union counterparts, Berdan's men.

PART 2
SHARPSHOOTER WEAPONS & TACTICS

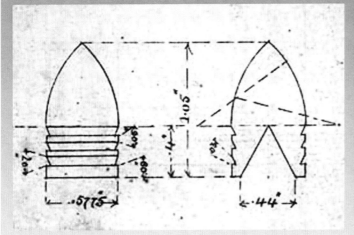

CHAPTER THREE

Confederate Sharpshooter Weapons and Equipment

ot long before the American Civil War, Europe's industrial revolution turned its irresistible momentum to firearms developments that would have a decisive impact on the American conflict. First came the percussion cap, which would render obsolete the Kentucky long rifle and its flint. Similar to a modern rifle primer, the percussion cap was a tiny copper cylinder containing a sensitive explosive powder—fulminate of mercury, charcoal, chlorate of potash, and ground glass that detonated when struck by a rifle's hammer. Invented by a Scottish Presbyterian minister, Alexander J. Forsyth, this tiny cap was slid atop a perforated nipple, which replaced the flintlock rifle's powder pan. Beneath the nipple, a small tube carried the hot flash into the rifle chamber. Instead of priming his pan, the rifleman simply slipped this metallic cap over the nipple.

Gone forever was the flintlock's old, *click!* . . . *sssss!* . . . *boom!*—replaced by a nearly instantaneous boom! This improved sharp-

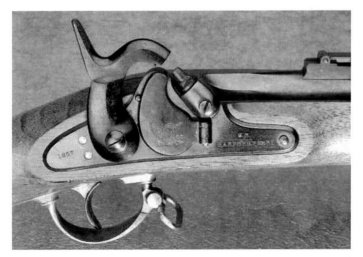

Slid over a rifle's metal nipple, the percussion cap represented a major improvement over the old flintlock's flint and powder pan ignition.

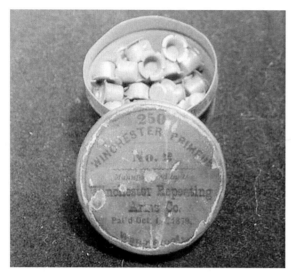

Pill-size percussion caps contained an explosive compound that detonated when struck by the rifle hammer, shooting a flash into the chamber. (Courtesy of Butch Holcombe, www.greybird relics.com.)

This "ladder-style" adjustable military rifle sight, circa 1845, allowed elevation tuning to 1,800 yards.

shooter marksmanship because it markedly reduced "lock time"—the time gap between pulling the trigger and a bullet exiting the muzzle—making a steady hold more easily accomplished. Further, British tests revealed, while a heavy trigger was needed to ensure sufficient sparks on a flintlock, on a percussion cap ignition system trigger pull could be lessened to 7 pounds with no decline in reliability, the lighter pull reducing the tendency to jerk a trigger.

Additionally, because the powder charge received a more consistent flash, muzzle velocity became more consistent, and hence, the rifle more accurate. Due to the efficiency of that flash, a percussion rifle required a smaller powder charge, about 25 percent less than a flintlock.

Resistance to rain and dampness, as well as firing reliability, improved markedly, too. Before the percussion cap's 1834 adoption by the British Army, 6000 rounds were fired in flintlock and percussion rifles. Some 922 times the flintlocks misfired or failed to fire while percussion caps failed only 36 times. Seven years later, the U.S. Army, too, switched to the percussion system for the 1841 or Mississippi Rifle. Many existing Kentucky long rifles were altered from flintlock to percussion.

ADJUSTABLE REAR SIGHT

About the same time another major improvement, the adjustable rear sight, first appeared on military weapons. Until the 1840s, long-range accuracy depended entirely upon a shooter's skill and experience, for he zeroed his rifle at a specific distance—usually 100 yards —and after that had to employ holdover ("Tennessee elevation") to hit targets at greater distances. A sharpshooter's ability to precisely compensate for range required years of experience.

Thanks to adjustable sights, a rifleman could now zero his rifle, then click or slide up its ladder-style elevation crossbar to aim directly at more distant targets with reasonable accuracy. The British Model 1851 Minie Rifle offered a graduated sight to 1,000 yards, while the 1853 Enfield went to 900 yards. Despite a degree of imprecision, compared to old-fashioned holdover, these sights advanced many a rifleman's abilities.

Not only did the adjustable sight allow better aiming, but once a rifleman found the proper range to, say, a row of approaching troops, he could shout his elevation to others and an entire squad or platoon thereby fire with reasonable accuracy.

MINIE BALL

The era's third major innovation was the Minie ball, a conical lead bullet designed by French Captain Claude-Etienne Minie in the 1840s, and improved on in Britain and America. Unlike a round lead ball, which required a strenuous effort to force down the bore and into the rifling, the pointed Minie projectile was slightly smaller than the bore because its thin, hollow base expanded into the rifling when fired.

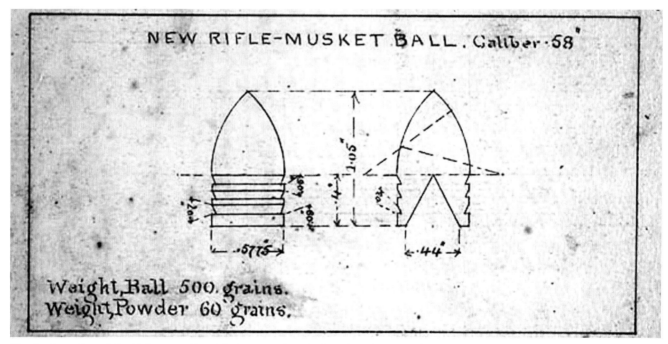

The final version of the U.S. .58-caliber Minie projectile, designed by James H. Burton at the Harpers Ferry Arsenal.

The Minie ball made reloading easier and faster. Gone was the need for patches because its three grooves held grease, which both lubricated the bore and formed a gas check when fired. Factory-made, the Minie came wrapped in waterproof paper with a standard powder charge; the rifleman tore open the paper, poured the powder in his bore, rammed the Minie ball home, slid a percussion cap on the nipple, and he was ready to fire. With Minie balls, he could fire and reload two or three rounds per minute. For the first time, riflemen had a firing rate equal to smoothbore shooters!

Ballistically, too, the Minie outclassed the round lead ball. Its streamlined, conical shape reduced drag, allowing the bullet to better retain velocity, thus flattening its trajectory and increasing its foot-pounds of energy delivered at longer ranges. Overall, this nearly doubled a rifle's maximum range, both for accuracy and lethality. A test firing in Britain demonstrated that a .577-caliber Minie ball at 800 yards could penetrate 4 inches of wood, an amazing performance.

The first military rifle to incorporate these cutting edge features—the percussion cap, pointed Minie ball, and adjustable rear sight—was the British Pattern 1851, but its inaccuracy soon gave way to the much superior Model 1853 Enfield, of .577 caliber. The first similar American arm, the 1861 Springfield rifle, fired a .58-caliber Minie ball, allowing ammunition interchangeability with the Enfield.

SHARPSHOOTER RIFLES

The most frequently employed sharpshooter weapon was the standard army rifle, most often the 1861 Springfield for Union troops and the British Model 1853 Enfield for Confederate soldiers. Due to recurring rifle shortages, however, it could have been either rifle.

Both were 9 1/2-pound muzzleloaders that incorporated adjustable sights, fired via a percussion cap, and shot Minie ball projectiles. In the hands of a competent infantryman, either rifle was capable of hitting a silhouette-size target at 250 yards; in the hands of a true marksman—such as a sharp-shooter—firing prone or from support, the range might double. But there were enough nuances between the two rifles that they did not perform identically at greater distances.

The Union Army's mainstay, the 1861 Springfield, was a reliable 56-inch-long workhorse with a 40-inch barrel in .58 caliber. Its considerable length was thought to make it a better weapon for bayonet fighting and confronting mounted cavalrymen. More than 1.5 million Springfields were manufactured in the North.

The Union Army's mainstay, the Model 1861 Springfield rifle.

The British Model 1853 "three-band" Enfield saw extensive service as a Confederate sharpshooter's rifle.

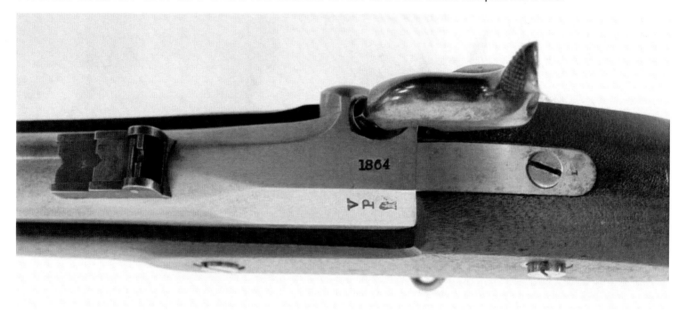

The Springfield's crude flip-up sight allowed shots at 100, 300, and 500 yards, with no adjustments for other distances.

An estimated 900,000 Model 1853 Enfield rifles made it past Union blockade ships to reach the hands of Confederate soldiers. The Enfield's barrel and overall length were 1 inch shorter than the Springfield's. The Confederate rifle's 530-grain Minie bullet left the muzzle at about 900 feet per second, roughly 50 feet per second slower than the Union rifle's 500-grain slug.

The most significant differences arose in their sights. While both had similar sight planes—that is, the distance between the front sight blade and rear sight—the adjustments were not similar. The earlier Springfield Model 1858 had sported a highly adjustable rear sight with a ladder-style crossbar allowing adjustments to 900 yards, which was simplified for the Model 1861. Thus Union soldiers

The Globe Target Sight

Many heavy-barreled Union sharpshooter rifles and Confederate Whitworths were not outfitted with scopes. A shortage of optical sights and their relatively high cost—$20 or more—compelled many sharpshooters to rely on globe target sights. And just as some rifles were called "telescope rifles" for their sighting system, these rifles were dubbed "globe rifles" or "globe-sighted rifles."

Actually, this term is a bit of a misnomer because "globe" refers only to the front sight, a short tube containing a fine peep or blade for exact aiming. The hood—like a modern rifle's hooded front sight—was designed to eliminate reflections and allow a crisper image for aiming. Some globe sights incorporated an integral spirit level so the shooter could watch its shifting bubble to make sure he wasn't canting—that is, he was not tipping the rifle down-right or down-left, which could cause his bullet to deviate right or left from his point of aim.

A precision globe sight with aiming insert atop a Whitworth barrel. Note the quality of the machining and the distinctive six-sided Whitworth rifling.

The accompanying rear sight was just as important. It was called a "tang" sight because it fit into the tang, the metal extension from the barrel that anchors it to the buttstock. The front globe sight could be drifted right or left in its dovetail during zeroing, but all the other fine adjustments for windage and elevation were accomplished using the tang sight. After achieving a solid zero, the sharpshooter minutely adjusted for each shot using micrometer-like tang sight adjustments, allowing precise shooting at long range.

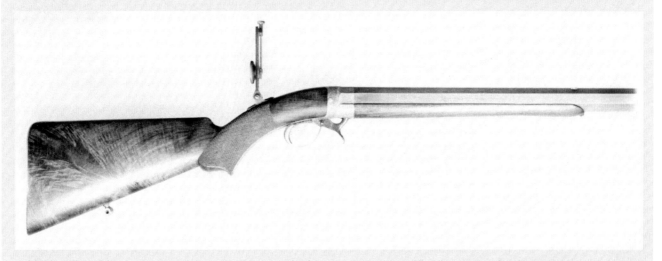

A highly adjustable tang target sight on a Warner under-hammer percussion rifle. (Courtesy of Robert Fisch.)

(and some sharpshooters) had Springfields with crude, flip-up rear sight blades for shooting 100, 300, and 500 yards. What was a Union sharpshooter to do when a Reb appeared at 365 yards—or 540 yards? He could only hold over or under and hope for the best.

By contrast, his Confederate counterpart, firing an Enfield rifle, knew what to do. His rifle sported flip-ups for fast firing at 100, 200, 300, and 400 yards, and an adjustable ladder-style sight to a maximum of 900 or even 1,250 yards, depending on the model. This advantage was not a minor one, for,

Precision Shooting with a Globe Sight

Just how accurate were Civil War sharpshooters' rifles when fired with globe sights? Historic accounts make all sorts of claims, some credible but many more not credible at all. Part of the difficulty in assessing accuracy is that modern standards for shooting and methods of measurement simply were not followed then. For instance, 150 years ago most target shooting was fired at 40 rods (220 yards), and groups were measured differently than today. U.S. and British government evaluations, too, had their own way of recording bullet impact—"deviation" it was called—which does not translate well.

I must thank the West Point Museum's former curator of arms, Robert Fisch, for assisting my research via his own .451-caliber under-hammer percussion rifle, believed built by Horace Warner, a Berdan Sharpshooter veteran. Although of conventional rifling, the Warner gun fires projectiles that are three times as long as their width, exactly as advised by Joseph Whitworth in 1855, and uses a globe front sight and tang rear sight. Fisch competed with this hexagonal-barreled rifle as a member of the United States International Muzzleloading Team from 1976 to 1983, earning world and international championships, as did his wife, Barbara.

And thanks to their experience, we can see what can be

Robert Fisch and his wife, Barbara, with their .451-caliber Warner target rifle and their championship 100-meter targets, fired with a globe sight. (Courtesy of Robert Fisch.)

achieved with a 19th-century .451-caliber rifle using a globe sight. Fisch put the Warner gun to good use at the 1980 World Championships, winning the Gold Medal for the aptly named Whitworth Match, with a score of 94 out of a possible 100—fired prone, with globe sight, at 100 meters (110 yards), using his own mechanically fitted bullets. Three years later he bettered that at an international match, scoring 98 out of 100; while at another match his wife, firing the Warner rifle, scored a 97. As you examine their photo, keep in mind that the 10 ring measures 1 15/16 inches, and I think you'll agree that a globe-sighted sharpshooter rifle was fully as precise a weapon as any scoped Civil War rifle, the only difference being magnification.

as any long-range shooter eventually realizes, *you cannot shoot more precisely than you can aim.*

Confederate sharpshooters went out of their way to fire only genuine Enfield .577-caliber Minie bullets—not .58-caliber Union rounds—which gave them better consistency from shot to shot. Such consistent performance from one shot to the next, they saw, was essential for achieving the greatest accuracy. Indeed, the Enfield-armed Rebel sharpshooters with Mahone's Brigade exclusively employed English-made slugs. "We never used any ammunition made by the Confederate government," wrote Captain John E. Laughton, General William Mahone's sharpshooter commander.

By most accounts and tests, the Enfield outshot the Springfield. In a side-by-side shoot-off, Confederate Major William Dunlop fired the British Minie rifle, the Enfield, the Springfield, and the 1841 "Mississippi Rifle," along with Austrian and Belgian guns. He concluded that while "each of them proved accurate and effective at short range, the superiority of the Enfield rifle for service at long range, from 600 to 900 yards, was clearly demonstrated, both as to force and accuracy of fire." The farthest the others could be relied on, Dunlop concluded, was 500 yards.

Firing a properly maintained Enfield, the 1860s British infantryman was expected to hit man-size targets half the time at 500 yards. The inventor of England's improved Minie bullet, R.T. Pritchett, firing at a 7-foot circular target at 500 yards, scored 98 hits of 100 rounds fired. These results are consistent with a 1971 test during which American rifleman Jac Weller fired 15 carefully loaded shots from an antique Enfield at 400 yards, scoring 13 hits into a 72-inch square target.

Two other factors, although unquantifiable, contributed to any rifle's long-range accuracy in the hands of a Civil War sharpshooter. The first factor was the rifle's quality of manufacture. Reflecting lower production rates and closer attention to detail, prewar or early-war rifles were better made than the later guns, meaning the rifling was crisper, the trigger smoother, the sight adjustments a hair more precise. Because they were hurried along in manufacturing, odds were that mid- and late-war rifles saw quality decline. In addition, the British Enfields were hand-finished, while the Springfields were not.

The second factor was the sharpshooter's familiarity with his rifle's idiosyncrasies. Had he mastered its distinct trigger pull? Did he know to "hold" it tight or loose? How true was his sight at each distance? Did he recognize and respect the tiny nuances that contributed to its unique "personality?" For good reason there's an old saying about riflemen: "Fear the man who owns only one gun." A sharpshooter who fired the same rifle, day-in, day-out, under all sorts of conditions—and heeded these experiences— learned to master his weapon in tiny but important ways that could not be taught in any class.

Such a man was Frank Bass, an Enfield-armed Confederate sharpshooter with the 7th Tennessee Regiment in Archer's Brigade. When a hidden Union sharpshooter shot several of Brigadier General James J. Archer's soldiers, Bass deliberately searched for him with binoculars until finally he spotted him "in a dense tree, protected by its body." An eyewitness recalled watching Bass "loading his Enfield carefully" and then stalking to an advantageous spot. "At the crack of Bass' gun," he continued, the well-concealed Union man "fell from the tree." On another day, it was Bass who was targeted and killed by "a long range shot" from a Union sharpshooter near Petersburg.

THE LEGENDARY WHITWORTH

Of all the Civil War sharpshooter's weapons, none equals the British-made Whitworth rifle—for

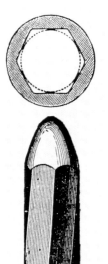

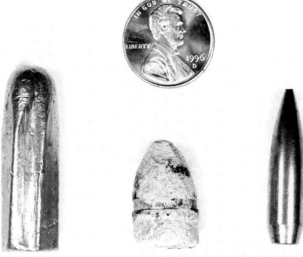

Far Left: The lengthy 530-grain Whitworth projectile, three times its diameter, and its distinctive six-sided bore.

Left: A hexagonal Whitworth bullet alongside a .52-caliber Sharps Minie ball and a modern .308-caliber 168-grain boattail bullet.

Right: Although marked "Manchester Ordnance and Rifle Company," this is a .451-caliber Whitworth with a tang rear sight.

Below: The Davidson rifle scope, visible on the left side of the receiver, required a peculiar body position. (Courtesy of the Virginia Historical Society.)

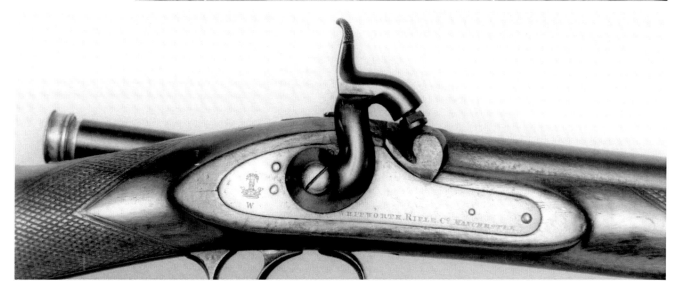

This Whitworth rifle, used by sharpshooter E.J. Gilbert, was topped by a Davidson's rifle scope. (Courtesy of the Virginia Historical Society.)

quality, accuracy, or reputation. And all of it is deserved.

From the hand-etched checkering on its stock to the buffed finish on its metal parts and the crisp precision of its micrometer-like adjustable sight, this rifle exudes confidence in its ability to place shots. Function-wise, it was hardly different from other muzzleloaders but for one feature: its unique, innovative projectile, a .451-caliber, six-sided bullet, actually a reverse image of the bore's hexagonal rifling (as seen on page 46).

Joseph Whitworth, a British mechanical genius, believed the Enfield rifle's .577-caliber Minie ball was "inefficient." After considerable research, he determined that a projectile's ideal proportions were a length three times that of its diameter. Long before the terms "sectional density" and "ballistic coefficient" were bandied about, Whitworth had determined that a javelin-shaped bullet was superior to stubby Minies. Thus, although both the Enfield .577-caliber and Whitworth .451-caliber bullets weighed 530 grains, the Whitworth "bolt" was three times longer and spun considerably faster with its rifling rate of one rotation per 20 inches. The implications for cutting through wind, for retaining velocity, for flat trajectory—they were all there. To Whitworth's disappointment, however, the British Ordnance Board rejected his superbly accurate rifle because it was less than .50 caliber and thus dubbed a "small bore" unsuitable for military use.

Undeterred, Whitworth put it into production as a target rifle, and that is what it was when discovered by Confederate arms purchasers in 1861. Despite its price—up to $1,000 with a Davidson scope and 1,000 rounds of ammunition—a handful were purchased and shipped to the South aboard a blockade runner. So impressive was their performance that a steady but small supply of Whitworth rifles reached the Confederate Army throughout the war. Some Whitworths, produced on license, bore the name "Thomas Turner Co.," while late-war rifles were labeled "Manchester Ordnance and Rifle Company," reflecting a reorganization of the Whitworth firm.

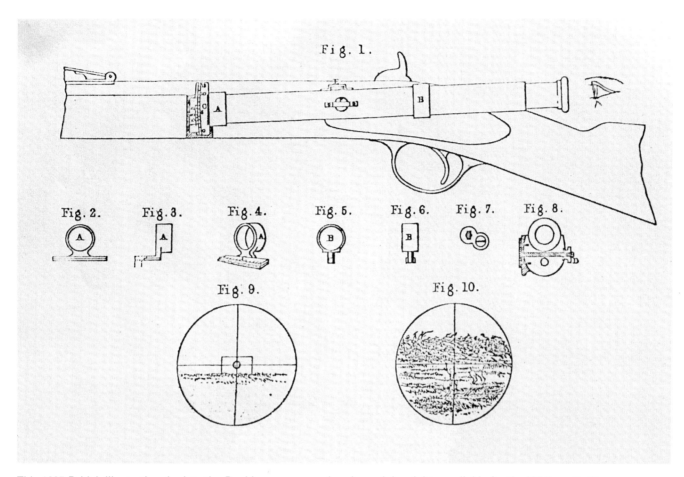

This 1865 British illustration depicts the Davidson scope and various globe sights available for the Whitworth rifle.

A precision Whitworth rear sight with hundredths-of-inch adjustments and ladder-style settings to 1,200 yards.

Civil War Scopes

The first major wartime use of the rifle scope, which in the 1860s was still a fairly new invention, occurred during the American Civil War by both Union and Confederate sharpshooters. What became the telescopic sight had begun about 50 years earlier as a lengthy tube down which a target shooter aimed. However, this "aiming tube" contained no lenses, only a crosshair made from fine wire or pig bristles. Eventually one version of the aiming tube would mature as the "globe sight," which is addressed on page 46.

Aiming through a magnifying lens can be traced back much further, to 1641, when a spider's web appeared in the telescope of William Gascoigne, an amateur astronomer. Gascoigne found it an excellent reference line for measuring heavenly bodies and soon was manufacturing them—but for astronomers, not riflemen.

The first American inventor to put magnifying lenses into a tube with a crosshair for aiming a rifle was John R. Chapman, in approximately 1835. Chapman, who described his invention in an 1844 book, *The Improved American Rifle,* assigned his patent rights to a Utica, New York, rifle builder, Morgan James. It was James, whose heavy rifles saw extensive service with Berdan's Sharpshooters, who put the first true rifle scopes into production. Another major scope maker of that era, William Malcolm

Lacking internal adjustments, this 19th-century scope's elevation and windage are controlled by finely threaded brass wheels.

of Syracuse, New York, also had optical sights on some sharpshooter rifles. Costing about $20 apiece with mounts, these mostly were low powered, probably on average 3x, but some, it is claimed, were 20x. Nearly all had brass tubes running the full length of the barrel.

Other than a focus knob, there were no moving parts, with all adjustments external, in the mounts. The front mount often was hinged, while the back mount contained fine adjustments for elevation and windage, usually as brass wheels or screws. In many cases, as in the photograph above, this rear mount was a rod and wheel assembly that passed through the buttstock at the pistol grip. Simple but effective, it shifted the entire scope slightly to shift the crosshairs.

Most optically fitted Confederate Whitworth rifles used the British-made Davidson Telescopic Rifle Sight, which may have predated the Chapman-James scope. Its inventor, British Army Lieutenant Colonel D. Davidson, claimed to have used his scope in India in 1835 "with singular success against the antelope on the Plains of the Deccan." Some 14 1/2 inches long with a 15/16-inch steel tube, the Davidson scope was mounted on the Whitworth receiver's left side, requiring Confederate sharpshooters to adopt a somewhat awkward body position when firing. Further, Whitworth sharpshooter veteran Stan C. Harley relates the scope's eye relief—the distance a shooter must hold his eye to see clearly through the scope—was so short that the scope often smacked the shooter's eye and, "the 'kick' being pretty hard, bruised the eye." British engineer William Ellis Metford soon fixed this problem by modifying the lens arrangement to widen eye relief "and so to escape damage from recoil."

Despite such early shortcomings, Lieutenant Colonel Davidson enthusiastically advocated his scope's use, writing,

Although it resembles a scope, this is an 1820s "aiming tube" on a flintlock target rifle.

Brass-tubed, barrel-length scopes atop 19-century target rifles: (top) a Warner under-hammer percussion rifle; (below) a Pennsylvania flintlock match rifle.

"Rifles fitted with telescopes would be of great value in rifle pits, in dislodging bushfighters, and in keeping down the fire of artillery."

To the uninformed, rifle scopes must have seemed a miraculous innovation that would make any rifleman a perfect marksman. The reality, however, was well expressed by a Berdan Sharpshooter who observed, "The crosswires within tremble so easily, that it requires a steady hand to hold the cross on the mark . . ." Yes, accurate shot placement still relied on the man behind the rifle, not a mechanical device.

All sported a 33-inch barrel with 48 3/4 inches overall length and a weight (without scope) 1 ounce short of 9 pounds, a half-pound lighter than the Enfield or Springfield. The rifle's tapered bore started at the breech, measuring .490 inch, and then tightened at the muzzle to .451 inch.

Many Whitworths were issued without scopes, but the rifle's excellent rear sight allowed surprisingly exact aiming. Since it was precision-machined from steel, its micrometer-like adjustments clicked off elevation in hundredths of an inch, while (alternately) the shooter could raise its crossbar using the other side of its scale to quickly elevate to 1,200 yards. Still other Whitworths came with target-style globe front sights and vernier rear sights, which offered even more precision.

The Whitworth in Action

The Whitworth round was supplied as a paper-wrapped cartridge to ensure a uniform quantity of powder. When rammed down the bore, an attached lubricating wad also coated the rifling. Sergeant Stan C. Harley, an Arkansas Whitworth sharpshooter, thought the six-sided bullet "looked fearfully long by the side of the short .58 caliber Minie bullet of the Enfield and Springfield rifles." Driven by a powder charge of "at least one hundred grains," the 530-grain Whitworth slug approximated the weight of a modern 12-

gauge shotgun slug, so stories about its considerable recoil are no exaggeration.

The terminal effect of Whitworth's streamlined heavy bullet was phenomenal. In British tests, fired at 307 yards, this bullet penetrated 33 half-inch elm planks, while a Sharps .52-caliber bullet cut through 18 boards and an Enfield just 15 boards.

And when it came to accuracy, there was simply no comparison with any existing military rifle. In 1857 trials at Britain's Hythe School of Musketry, a Whitworth and an Enfield Model 1853 each fired 10 rounds from a mechanical rest at 500, 800, 1,100, 1,400, and 1,800 yards, recording the "average of divergence." Unlike measuring groups today, this meant measuring how far each round impacted from dead-center and then averaging the total impacts. For example, when one bullet impacted 2 inches from center, and the next hit 4 inches from center, the average divergence for the two was 3 inches. The Hythe results were as follows:

AVERAGE DIVERGENCE (INCHES)

	500 Yards	800 Yards	1,100 Yards	1,400 Yards	1,800 Yards
Whitworth	4.4	12	29	55	139
Enfield	28.8	49	96	No Hits	No Hits

As was noted in 1857, the Whitworth at 1,100 yards was as accurate as an Enfield at 500 yards. Analyzing these figures, I noticed that the Whitworth group widened disproportionately with range, increasing from less than 1 minute of angle (MOA) at 500 yards to 7.7 minutes of angle at 1,800 yards. This reflected, I think, the effect of a bit of crosswind and the lower magnification and lens quality of that era's rifle scopes, not the rifle.

Where it really mattered—in the hands of a sharpshooter, not a mechanical firing rest—the Whitworth demonstrated similar accuracy. A *Charleston Mercury* article of 13 June 1864 reported that a Whitworth-armed sharpshooter was "so skilled that in the presence of that general [Ewell] he put seventeen balls in succession in a space no larger than the hand, at the distance of 500 yards."

To maintain such accuracy, the rifle required at least a quick swabbing every few rounds, plus a detailed cleaning probably every day.

Due to the Whitworth's high cost and the difficulties of running the Union Navy's blockade, there never was a large supply of these phenomenal rifles. During the Atlanta Campaign, the Confederacy's

A 10-round box of Whitworth paper-wrapped cartridges, as issued to Confederate sharpshooters. (Image from the Military and Historical Image Bank.)

Army of the Tennessee had but 26 Whitworth sharpshooter rifles out of 49,303 shoulder arms. General Joseph Johnston's army, attempting to ward off Grant's attack on Vicksburg, received just 20 Whitworths. Major General William Bate's division had only one squad of Whitworth sharpshooters, led by Lieutenant A.B. Schell. Georgia sharpshooter Berry Benson's entire brigade possessed just one Whitworth rifle. "It was presented to (Ben) Powell," he wrote in his diary, "as he was known to be an excellent shot."

You can only imagine the competition among sharpshooters for these precious few rifles. "We all wanted the gun," explained Confederate sharpshooter Sam R. Watkins. "All the generals and officers came out to see us shoot. The mark was put up about 500 yards on a hill, and each of us had three shots. Every shot that was fired hit the board, but there was one man who came a little closer to the spot than any other, and the Whitworth was awarded to him." The First Tennessee Regiment conducted a similar shoot-off, with a target 800 yards away. The winner was William Beasley, who put three shots out of five in a man-size target.

"The terrible effect of such weapons," a sharpshooter in General Patrick Cleburne's division wrote, "in the hands of men who had been selected, one only from each infantry brigade because of his special merit as a soldier and his skill as a marksman, can be imagined." Such a soldier was Sergeant John H.W. Terry of the Second Tennessee Infantry, who from the 6 April 1862 Battle of Shiloh until he was severely wounded at Kennesaw Mountain on 20 September 1864, carried and fired a Whitworth rifle through fights and skirmishes too numerous to detail.

THE KERR SHARPSHOOTER'S RIFLE

Another British muzzleloading target rifle that resembled the Whitworth, the Kerr rifle also saw considerable service as a Confederate sharpshooter's weapon. Designed by James Kerr as a target rifle

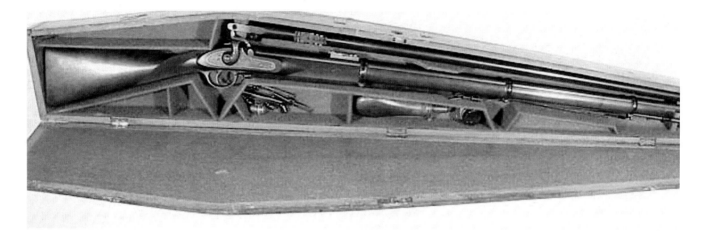

A boxed British-made Kerr .451-caliber sharpshooter's rifle, a precision contemporary of the famed Whitworth rifle.

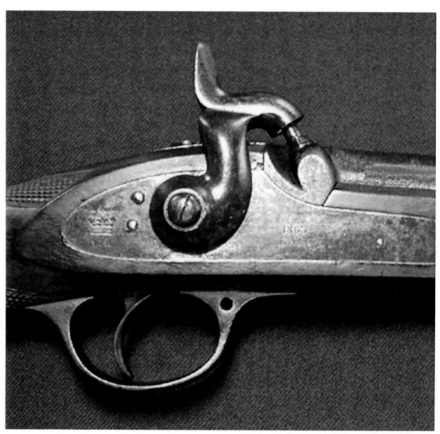

Above: The Kerr rifle's lock resembles the Whitworth's, of which it was a licensed clone.

Left: The Kerr rifle's sight is finely graduated to 1,000 yards.

for shooting 1,000 yards or farther, it was topped by high-quality sights and required special, high-grade gunpowder for top performance. The London Armoury Company manufactured the Kerr.

Of similar .451 caliber (or .466 Kerr caliber), it fired the Whitworth-style elongated hexagonal projectile. A bit longer overall at 53 inches, it employed a slightly shorter barrel. According to Ed

Thompson of the Orphan Brigade, the Kerr rifle "would kill at the distance of a mile or more, requiring a peculiar powder; and there was some difficulty in charging it, so that it was not likely to be fully effective except in the hands of a cool and composed man."

The Kerrs were competed for and issued on a basis similar to the Whitworths, with, for example, 11 Kerr rifles issued to the finest marksmen in the Orphan Brigade for the 1864 Atlanta Campaign. Interestingly, Captain A. Buck Schell, a sharpshooter commander in Cleburne's division, wrote that his unit's Kerr rifles had been "made in [the] arsenal at Macon, Georgia." Some historians believe Schell was mistaken or that these were repaired rifles, but I think he may have been correct, the rifles having been built from imported British-made barrels, locks, and sights. My evidence is found in the Columbus, Georgia, municipal museum and is explained below.

OTHER CONFEDERATE SHARPSHOOTER RIFLES

During a visit to the U.S. Army Sniper School at Fort Benning, I toured the municipal museum in nearby Columbus, Georgia. In a display case, at first I thought I'd found a finely crafted Whitworth rifle—labeled a Confederate sharpshooter's weapon—but I was completely wrong. At the outbreak of the Civil War, the Columbus gunmaking firm of Greenwood & Gray employed as lead gunsmith J.P. Murray, who was renowned for building match-grade target rifles. With the coming of war, he turned his efforts to sharpshooter rifles, including the outstanding specimen displayed in the museum. Although of conventional rifling, this Murray rifle proved that the South possessed expert craftsmen

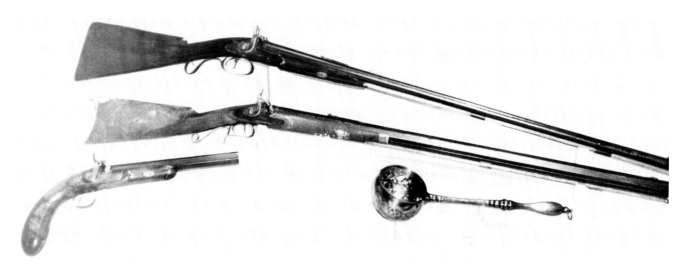

This Confederate sharpshooter's rifle (center), displayed at the Columbus, Georgia, city museum, was handcrafted by J.P. Murray.

capable of building superbly accurate rifles, whether from scratch or from imported parts. And Murray was hardly alone.

In New Orleans, Cook & Brother Manufacturing produced high-quality, heavy-barreled target rifles, offering precision sights and finely tuned triggers. The Morse target rifle, custom built in Richmond, Virginia, was of such quality that it demanded $150 in gold. The E.H. Rogers Company in Augusta, Georgia, built octagon-barreled target rifles, complete with double set triggers. In Montgomery, Alabama, German-born master gunsmith Christian Kreutner countersunk his target rifle muzzles as bullet starters and normally installed double set triggers. Another German emigré, George Balzer, settled in Hayneville, Alabama, and built similar high-quality target rifles before and during the Civil War. Phillip Betis of Vickery Creek, Georgia, also constructed custom target-grade rifles that undoubtedly saw service as Confederate sharpshooter weapons.

Though I've not had the opportunity to test-fire any of these custom rifles, I would expect that they proved as accurate as their Northern counterpart "telescope" rifles, making them 1,000-yard guns.

CHAPTER FOUR

Union Sharpshooter Weapons and Equipment

U nlike the South's limited industrial base, which created a need for foreign-made sharpshooter weapons, the North possessed a mature firearms industry capable of supplying or developing arms for Union sharpshooters. Berdans Sharpshooters had both an issued standard military rifle, and a heavy rifle available as needed. When called on to make an especially long shot, a Union sharpshooter could swap his day-to-day rifle for a heavy-barreled, scoped rifle, referred to in the 1860s as "telescope rifles"—or in sharpshooter slang "artillery, as the boys call them."

The Morgan James trigger, lock, and scope elevation wheel display as much precision as the rifle itself. (Courtesy of the West Point Museum.)

There was no standard heavy rifle. The most common one, manufactured by Morgan James, incorporated a thick, octagonal barrel, typically weighing 30 to 32 pounds. In 1860, a Morgan James target rifle cost $95 with scope and reloading tools. The .50-caliber Morgan James rifle belonging to New York sharpshooter J.C. Nobel, displayed at the Infantry Museum at Fort Benning, Georgia, fitted with a barrel-length telescopic sight, weighed only

The Morgan James "telescope rifle," the Union Army's tack-driving, long-range sharpshooting rifle. (Courtesy of the West Point Museum.)

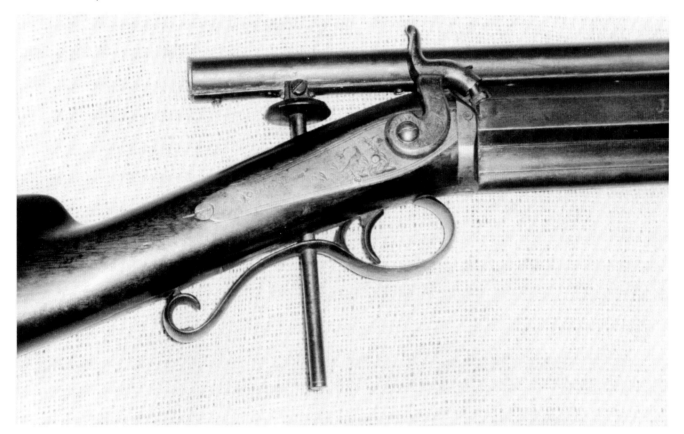

Displayed at the Fort Benning Infantry Museum, this .50-caliber telescope rifle belonged to Private J.C. Nobel of Company G, 1st Battalion, New York Sharpshooters.

A precision 1860s target rifle built by S.C. Miller.

The First Scoped Rifle Engagement

The American Civil War saw the first major wartime use of rifle scopes, but it was probably not the first time optical sights had seen military action. Various sources allege that British officers employed privately acquired scoped rifles while quelling India's Sepoy Mutiny in 1857. Lieutenant Colonel D. Davidson, the British officer-inventor of the scope bearing his name, circumstantially supports this possibility, reporting in 1865 that British officers in India had his scopes 15 years earlier. I have yet to find actual documentation that one of these rifles saw combat action.

Five years earlier, however, there's a well-documented account of a Wesson target rifle being fired with dramatic effect in New Mexico. This short engagement, in June 1851, was fired at long range, although there's no specific mention of the type of sight on the heavy-barreled rifle. Trouble arose when a U.S. Boundary Commission Survey Team, escorted by Lieutenant Amiel Weeks Whipple and a detachment of soldiers, encountered a party of Apache raiders. Giving chase, Weeks and his men found themselves delayed by a rear guard whose leader took delight in exposing his buttocks and mocking them. The warrior, a Mangas Coloradas Apache named Delgadito, thought he was beyond rifle range; what he did not know was that one of Lieutenant Whipple's men, a teamster named Wells, was a superb shot, and he had a heavy-barreled Wesson target rifle. Taking careful aim, Wells fired, placing his shot exactly where he intended, causing "an unearthly yell and a series of dances and capers that would put a *maitre de ballet* to blush." Lieutenant Whipple and his men must have chuckled for some time. There is, however, more to this story.

Amiel Weeks Whipple was present at the 1851 scoped-rifle engagement; 12 years later, as a Union major general, he appeared in a Rebel sharpshooter's scope.

Twelve years later, midway in the Civil War at the Battle of Chancellorsville, this same lieutenant was a hardened veteran and wore two stars on his collar. On 4 May 1863, Major General Whipple, now a division commander, was called over by General Daniel Sickles and told to bring in the Berdan Sharpshooters to silence a squad of Confederate sharpshooters who had been suppressing the Union artillery.

Sitting atop his horse, Whipple was writing the order when a single long-range bullet struck him, throwing him to the ground. Arriving on the scene, a detachment of Berdan's men returned fire and were credited with shooting "five of the [Rebel] sharpshooters," including the one suspected of having shot General Whipple.

But it was too late. For Whipple—the officer who had overseen what was probably the first long-range scoped rifle engagement in history—had died at the hands of a distant sharpshooter.

A scoped Wesson target rifle, similar to that fired in June 1851 at a hostile Apache, quite possibly history's first scoped rifle engagement.

Sharpshooter Glasses

Some Civil War sharpshooters wore a peculiar optical aid to assist their shooting: orthoptic spectacles. Although they resemble ordinary shaded sunglasses, on closer inspection it's apparent that only the center of each lens allows a clear view, while the rest of the lens is cloudy or dulled.

"The principle of the orthoptic is the focusing of the field of vision before it reaches the lens of the eye," explains a 19th-century shooting guide. "The advantage is better definition, especially of the fore-sight and bull's-eye." You can test the effectiveness of this yourself by punching a tiny hole through a piece of paper and looking through it, which should yield a crisper view than with normal eyesight. Orthoptic glasses were especially useful, it was believed, when firing a globe-sighted rifle.

The U.S. Army's Infantry Museum at Fort Benning, Georgia, includes in its collection a pair of these unusual spectacles, used during the Civil War by Private J.C. Nobel, a Union sharpshooter, whose rifle also is on display.

Orthoptic glasses allowed a Civil War sharpshooter to better focus his eyes. Note the clear lens centers.

13 pounds. A variety of Northerners built similar rifles, such as R.R. Moore of Courtlandt Street in New York, whose .52-caliber target rifle had a heavy 30-inch barrel. Although primarily producing pistols, Colt, too, hand-built heavy-barreled target rifles in .54 caliber, weighing nearly 23 pounds. The heaviest sharpshooter target rifle I've come upon is the Abe Williams heavy bench rifle, which weighed an astonishing 57 pounds.

Virtually all the Berdan Sharpshooter heavy rifles were privately owned, brought along by volunteers who eventually learned there was nothing to the government's promise of $60 reimbursement for each target rifle. Bitterly, some sharpshooters laughed that "USSS" stood for "Unfortunate Souls, Shrewdly Sold."

Once the U.S. sharpshooters were issued Colt rifles, their heavy target weapons were collected and stored in the unit wagon train. "The giving of these telescopic rifles but few of which were now carried . . . was in the nature of a mark of honor," explained the Berdan unit history, "as the sharpshooter thus armed was considered an independent character, used only for special service, with the privilege of going to any part of the line where in his own judgment he could do the most good.

"The 'telescopic' men were supposed to perform the fine work of the regiment, such as making close [difficult] shots at long range," the history continues, "using their telescopes to make objects dim to the naked eye, perfectly plain and distinct, and some exciting specimens of marksmanship was the result."

FIRING THE HEAVY RIFLES

The great accuracy of heavy rifles resulted as much from deliberation in loading as in precise aiming and firing. Supplied with each rifle was a "false muzzle," a severed section of the original barrel—about 4 inches long—that precisely aligned to the bore with four projecting metal pins. When loading, this false muzzle was attached to protect the crown—the edge of the rifling where the bullet exits—to preclude even the tiniest nick from degrading accuracy by disrupting the bullet's passage. The false muzzle also ensured that the tight-fitting projectile entered the rifling straight and true when the sharpshooter tapped it in using a plunger or small mallet. Once the bullet was a couple of inches into the rifling, the sharpshooter removed the false muzzle and finished seating it with a ramrod.

In addition to false muzzles, many target rifles had double, or "set," triggers. In this arrangement, one trigger is actually a lever that "sets" the second, more sensitive trigger, which offers so little resistance that it can be tripped with a hair—a "hair trigger." The belief was that a rifle requiring only the

Some heavy sharpshooter's rifles employed open, or "globe," sights, like this Andrews Sharpshooter's long-range rifle. (Image from the Military and Historical Image Bank.)

Union sharpshooter Charles Rice holds an octagon-barrel, heavy target rifle. (Courtesy of the Archives of Michigan.)

Many heavy rifles required a false muzzle (left) to ensure that the bullet aligned with the rifling and a mallet (right) to force it down. Reloading was cumbersome and slow.

slightest touch to fire imparted no movement from the shooter's finger and thus fired more accurately.

As far as accuracy, there's no question that these were the most accurate rifles of their day. In 1859, Morgan James personally shot a 25-round demonstration at 220 yards, with all 25 shots impacting within 1.4 inches of dead-zero, meaning a 2.8-inch-wide group. That same year in another demonstration, James fired nine shots at 110 yards, yielding a group measuring just 0.38 inch—virtually one ragged hole.

Similarly, the first annual National Rifle Club's competition in October 1859 was won by Mr. T. Spencer, also firing 50 rounds from a heavy-barreled target rifle at 220 yards, which yielded a 2.16-inch group. In a 600-yard demonstration of his personal scoped target rifle—apparently a Morgan James—Colonel Hiram Berdan "put five consecutive shots within the ten-inch ring."

Even President Lincoln tried out a heavy target rifle, belonging to Private Harrison Peck of the 1st U.S. Sharpshooter Regiment, during a September 1861 visit to the Berdan's training camp. "Abraham Lincoln handled the rifle like a veteran marksman," reported the *New York Herald*, and he told onlookers, "Boys, this reminds me of old time shooting."

The upside of these heavy rifles was their accuracy, but there were downsides, too. Private William Fletcher, a superb Confederate marksman, after looking over his division's heavy rifles, reckoned he did not want one, announcing, "I would not accept one if offered, for I did not think they were a good brush gun or one that could be dragged around on a crawl." Union sharpshooter Captain Charles Stevens agreed on the heavy rifle's limited usefulness, explaining, "The muzzle-loading target rifles—telescopic and globe-sighted—while of great value before fortifications and for special work, would have been useless in skirmishing."

With their tight tolerances, these heavy rifles also proved more temperamental than other weapons, especially their susceptibility to black powder fouling. Accuracy declined after only four or five rounds, and a few rounds later it became difficult to force balls down the fouled bore. Indeed, even when freshly cleaned, these rifles offered a rate of fire slower than a Kentucky Long Rifle. That reality led to disaster on 17 September 1862, at the Battle of Antietam, where two companies of Massachusetts sharpshooters were armed solely with heavy target rifles. Unable to reload quickly, 26 sharpshooters were cut down in a single day.

THE COLT REVOLVING RIFLE

Realizing that these heavy rifles were not suited to everyday skirmishing and scouting, Colonel Berdan sought a more appropriate weapon. Thus as a stopgap until better rifles were available, his two sharpshooter regiments were armed with the Colt Model 1855 revolving rifle, a .56-caliber five-shooter, looking like a stretched cap-and-ball revolver. Weighing 10 1/2 pounds with a 37 1/2-inch barrel and overall length of 55 inches, the Colt revolving rifle was 1 inch shorter than the Springfield.

Private Chauncey Maltby, Company B, 2nd U.S. Sharpshooters, with his Colt Revolving rifle.

Bureaucratic inertia delayed acquisition of the Colt rifles, mostly due to the chief of ordnance, General James W. Ripley, an obstinate old man who refused to consider acquiring any weapon except the standard Model 1861 Springfield, of which he'd been the greatest advocate. President Lincoln finally had to countermand Ripley, ordering, "Let it [the purchase] be executed at once."

Originally produced in 1836, the Colt rifle is surrounded by many exaggerations. The 1864 book *Hints to Riflemen* claimed this Colt rifle was accurate to 680 yards, while another book, *The Rifle and How to Use It*, praised it as "the best military arm" produced up to that time. Neither claim was even close to the truth.

"They were five-chambered breech loaders, very pretty to look at, but upon examination and test they were found inaccurate and unreliable, prone to get out of order and even dangerous to the user," wrote sharpshooter Wyman S. White. Berdan's men appreciated the benefits of a breechloading, five-shot repeater, but loading was a slow, tedious process, requiring each of the five chambers to be loaded separately.

A clear summary of its shortcomings is contained in a letter from sharpshooter Theodore Preston, who observed, "[First] it is too light for the size and weight of the lead [projectile]. Second, when the ball leaves the cylinder and enters the barrel, there are small shavings of lead [that] escape from between the cylinder and the barrel, and fly six or eight feet, endangering a person." And, according to another sharpshooter, "there was some danger of all the chambers exploding at once." One man lost a thumb and forefinger to an exploding Colt rifle.

Still, that five-shot capacity could come in handy. On one occasion a handful of Colt-armed sharpshooters warded off a large Confederate assault by the *sound* of their five-shooters rapidly firing, giving the impression that the Rebs had tangled with a much larger force.

THE SHARPS RIFLE

Hiram Berdan's Sharpshooters used those Colt rifles for only about six months while he arranged for a more capable, permanent weapon. His final decision undoubtedly was influenced by Sergeant Truman "California Joe" Head, who had purchased a Sharps Model 1859 rifle from a company sales representative in September 1861. Once California Joe was sold on its favorable qualities, it took little to convince Berdan that the Sharps was the best rifle for his men.

Employing a falling or sliding block action (operating a bit like a lever gun), the breechloading, .52-caliber Sharps rifle used bullets wrapped in linen or paper cartridges, making it extremely fast to load. It weighed 8 3/4 pounds and measured 47 inches overall with a 30-inch barrel, and typically fired a 350-grain bullet. (Contrary to what you may have heard, the word *sharpshooter* does not come from this rifle. That term had existed for 100 years, long before the rifle's inventor, Christian Sharps, was born.)

As with the Colt rifle, Berdan had to request the Sharps through the chief of ordnance, General Ripley, renowned as "the father of the muzzle-loading Springfield rifle." Ripley refused the

The Sharps action and set triggers. Rotating downward, the trigger guard opened the breech for inserting a combustible paper cartridge.

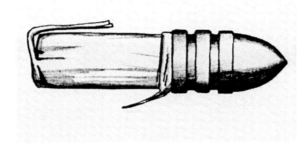

Treated with potassium nitrate, the paper-wrapped .52-caliber Sharps cartridge was quick to load and totally consumed in firing.

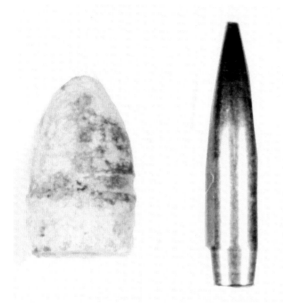

A recovered .52-caliber Sharps bullet, found at Gettysburg, alongside a modern .308-caliber, 168-grain, boattail hollowpoint.

request. Then Berdan sent California Joe and his Sharps rifle to Secretary of War Simon Cameron and followed up with a letter, telling Cameron, "The men as well as myself feel that with these weapons we can not only make a name for ourselves but be of vast service to the country."

Even with Cameron's approval, the obstinate General Ripley stalled, causing a New York newspaper to note, "Sharps rifles were promised to them by the President and ordered by General McClellan, but some trouble in the War Department has thus far prevented them getting them." Eventually the rifles were ordered, and afterward the crotchety General Ripley, famous as the ordnance chief "who combated all new ideas," was forced into retirement.

The Sharps rifle version delivered to the U.S. Sharpshooters incorporated several significant modifications requested by Berdan. First, he eliminated the bayonet lug on the barrel, which probably enhanced barrel harmonics and also conveniently precluded his men being called on to assault like line infantry. The single trigger was replaced with a set-trigger system, and the

A typical Sharps breechloading rifle with set triggers. This rifle was used by Berdan Sharpshooter George Albee, who was later awarded the Medal of Honor for an Indian Wars action. (Courtesy of West Point Museum.)

standard rear sight was replaced with a finer one offering precise adjustments to 1,000 yards. The complete rifle cost $42.50—more than twice the price of a Springfield.

The only Civil War accuracy test I've found for the Model 1859 Sharps involved five rifles firing linen-wrapped cartridges. At 500 yards, these rifles scored 24 hits of 25 rounds fired, but the report didn't cite the target's size. More recently, a black powder shooter, Andy Moe, extensively tested carefully wrapped .52-caliber paper cartridges in a reproduction Sharps carbine. Moe's 2004 test, fired at 30 yards from a sandbag rest, produced five-shot groups measuring 1/2 to 3/4 inch, which would equate to about 1 1/2 inches at 100 yards—certainly accuracy worthy of a sharpshooter.

Berdan's men received their first Sharps rifle in mid-May 1862, and by mid-June both regiments were fully armed.

The Sharps Rifle in Action

The Sharps rifle proved fast to load and reliable to operate. To load, the sharpshooter grasped the extended trigger guard—which operates as a lever—and swung it forward to open the breech and allow a paper- or linen-wrapped cartridge to be inserted. Then he simply rotated back the trigger guard to both close the action and cut off the back of the cartridge, exposing the powder. By simply cocking the hammer and sliding a percussion cap over the nipple, he was ready to fire.

Each sharpshooter carried sixty .52-caliber paper cartridges as his basic load, with 10 rounds per cardboard package, which included 12 percussion caps. The paper or linen wrappings were combustible, having been treated with potassium nitrate, leaving minimal residue in the chamber.

If the sharpshooter was hurried, he could fire immediately by pulling the rear of the two triggers. For more deliberate shots, he first pulled the forward trigger to set the rear trigger, reducing it to a "hair" trigger—ready to trip with a slight touch.

The Berdan version of the 1859 Sharps proved a superb sharpshooter's and skirmisher's rifle. Because it was a breechloader, the shooter did not have to ram a rod down the muzzle, allowing him to load efficiently while

Proudly posing with his Sharps rifle, Private William Henderson served in Company K, 1st U.S. Sharpshooter Regiment.

Range Estimation in the 1860s

Several range-measuring devices were invented in Britain in the 1850s. One device featured a piece of brass sheet metal with a wedge cut out of it, along the edge of which were lines indicating distances. Holding this "stadium" device exactly 22 2/3 inches from his eye—accomplished by holding taut a cord of that length—the sharpshooter carefully held the wedge opening over a man until the opening was just as wide as the man was tall, and read the indicated distance. Given the natural variations in human height and the tiny angular differences between, say, a man 500 yards away and another 600 yards away, you can see why it was not considered very accurate. A copy of this device was manufactured at the U.S. Frankford Arsenal during the Civil War.

Holtzapffel & Company of London manufactured a slightly more refined device (illustrated here), which was issued to some Confederate sharpshooters. Employed similarly to the other stadium (a taut cord held exactly 25 inches from the eye), it measured

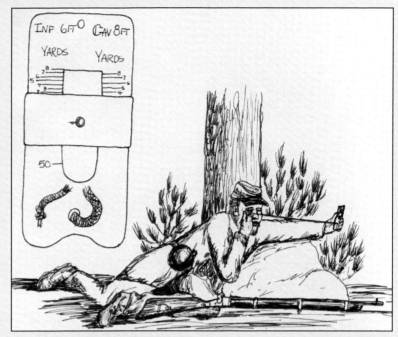

Holding a stadium ranging device exactly 25 inches from his eye, a Confederate sharpshooter could measure targets up to 800 yards away. (Original art by Tami Anderson.)

dismounted and mounted enemy with a sliding bar that more precisely assessed target height. To fine-tune it, the shooter changed the cord length to better fit the length of his arm and eyesight. This Holtzapffel device could range up to 800 yards, but after 500 yards the increments became so tiny that significant error inevitably arose. Still, it was a step forward from the Revolutionary War, in which the only ranging device was a human thumb held at arm's length.

lying behind cover. Further, the combination of prewrapped combustible cartridges and self-priming enhanced his rate of fire; in fact, a sharpshooter could fire up to 10 aimed rounds per minute, about triple the rate of a muzzleloader. Add to this the Sharps' quality, adjustable sights and set triggers, and it made for a very effective weapon.

"The possession of these rifles," concluded sharpshooter Wyman White, "made every man in the regiment a Sharpshooter, in fact, and the men with their little Sharps made their mark wherever and whenever they came in contact with the Rebels."

This is borne out by Colonel William F. Fox's authoritative *Regimental Losses in the American Civil War*, which concluded:

> "Berdan's United States Sharp-Shooters . . . were continually in demand as skirmishers on account of their wonderful proficiency as such, and they undoubtedly killed more men than any other regiment in the army. In skirmishing they had no equal."

RIFLES OF THE WESTERN SHARPSHOOTERS

Members of the Union Army's other major sharpshooter organization, Birge's Western Sharpshooters, also were issued a rifle unique to their unit. At first this was the Dimick American Deer and Target Rifle, a heavy-barreled muzzleloader. Horace Dimick's St. Louis shop could not handle the huge demand, so several arms makers built his rifle on contract. Eventually, 1,000 Dimick rifles armed the Western Sharpshooters.

Considered a Plains rifle, the Dimick had been around for several years, with a primary role of long-range shooting against large game, especially buffalo. With its heavy octagonal barrel, the gun weighed approximately 12 pounds, although its half stock gave it a sportier look and feel. Some were supplied with double set triggers, but most of those in sharpshooters' hands had a single trigger.

The Dimick sharpshooter's rifle fired a .44-caliber bullet dubbed a Swiss Chasseur, a hollow-based, conical variety of Minie ball popular in Europe and often fired by German target rifles. Another Dimick rifle, popular among adventurers passing through St. Louis to try their stake as mountain men, was bored in .52 caliber.

Lorenzo Barker, a Birge's Western Sharpshooter veteran who authored his unit's history, recalled:

> "The [rifle's] accoutrements were not the kind prescribed by army regulations; but, consisted of a bullet pouch of bear skin covering and a powder horn, or in some cases a flask. In the bullet pouch was a compartment where the soldier carried his screw drivers, bullet molds and patch cutter, singular implements for the soldier; but, Birge's boys molded their own bullets, greased them, and patched them with as much care as an old hunter would and used them as effectively."

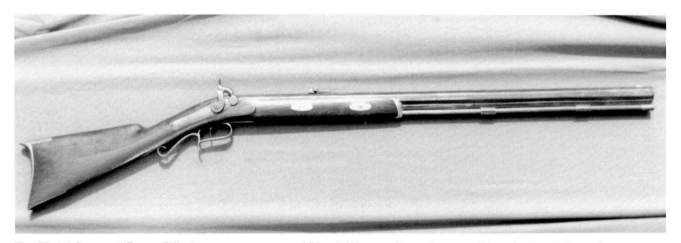

The Dimick Deer and Target Rifle, long-range weapon of Birge's Western Sharpshooters. (Photo by Dan P. Fagen.)

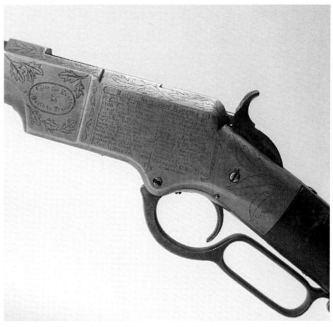

Birge's Western Sharpshooters with Dimick Deer and Target Rifles. (Richard F. Carlile Collection.)

Western Sharpshooter Lorenzo Barker's highly engraved Henry rifle is displayed at the Michigan Historical Museum in Lansing. (Photo by Johnny Quirin for *Michigan History Magazine*.)

One Western Sharpshooter, Amariah Spencer, boasted to his family that "our guns will carry from 600 to one thousand yards," while his own rifle fired "1/2 oz. balls and will carry 400 yards with level sites [*sic*]."

THE HENRY LEVER-ACTION RIFLE

Long-range precision fire was useful, but many Western Sharpshooters found that their most frequent skirmishing encounters were at medium or close range, and only rarely over 200 yards. In such circumstances, the sharpshooters began to realize, their shooting required no more accuracy than an ordinary rifle, while their Dimick rifles' heavy weight and low rate of fire put them at a disadvantage. As skirmishers—which, like Berdan's Sharpshooters, was their most frequent role—they would be better served by a lighter rifle offering more firepower. However, they did not choose the Sharps rifle. Instead, late in 1863 the Western Sharpshooters decided that the Henry lever-action would be an ideal skirmishing weapon.

Just like the Sharps rifle, this weapon choice found no support in the War Department. Instead of trying to politically end-run the chief of ordnance like Berdan had done, however, the sharpshooters

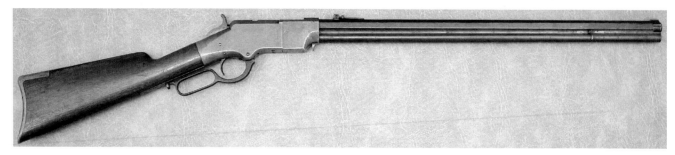

The Henry rifle, a fast-firing 17-shooter, was so valued by the Western Sharpshooters that the whole regiment bought their own guns with their own money.

Although its sight was optimistically graduated to 900 yards, the Henry rifle's realistic maximum range was about 200 yards.

found a novel alternative—they reached into their own pockets, anteing up $42 apiece, *one-quarter of a year's pay*, to buy the rifles. While the entire Union Army acquired only 1,731 Henry lever guns during the war, the Western Sharpshooters alone purchased 1,000 Henrys.

These revolutionary lever-action repeaters also fired revolutionary ammunition—first-generation metallic cartridges, chambered for the .44 Henry rimfire round. Much like a modern .22 Long Rifle round, the .44 Henry cartridge contained an explosive powder folded into its rim that would explode when struck by a firing pin. Since the cartridge was entirely self-contained, the sharpshooter needed no percussion cap, no powder to pour, and no bullet to ram. He simply dropped 16 rounds down the tubular magazine below the barrel and levered the action, and he was ready to fire. Confederate soldiers soon called it "that damned Yankee rifle that's loaded on Sunday and fired all week." The Henry rifle weighed 9 1/4 pounds, incorporating a 24-inch barrel with 44 3/4 inches overall length.

The First Periscope Rifle

The deadly attentiveness of World War I snipers made it nearly suicidal for a soldier to raise his head above a parapet. Necessity created a novel solution—a periscope mounted on a rifle's butt—so riflemen could aim and fire from safety. Historians pretty well accept that this innovation first saw light in the trenches of Western Europe, circa 1915. Actually, the periscope rifle dates back at least to June 1864, when Colonel Ellison Capers of the 24th South Carolina Volunteers encountered one near Marietta, Georgia. So impressed was he by this clever device that he had it entered in a regimental report:

> "In the fight of the 24th we captured a sharpshooter who had a small looking-glass attached to the butt of his musket, so that he could sit behind his breast-work, perfectly protected, with his back to us, and by looking into his glass, sight along the barrel of his piece."

This periscope probably sprang from one sharpshooter's ingenuity, for nowhere in Civil War records have I found any reference to one, either as a manufactured device or an item issued to sharpshooters.

The .44 Henry's 200-grain bullet, propelled by 26 to 28 grains of black powder, made it only a moderately powerful round of limited range. Yet its ladder-style rear sight optimistically allowed aimed fire to 900 yards, which caused me to do a bit of research. Assuming a 1,050 feet per second muzzle velocity and 100-yard zero, I ran the .44 Henry through my Sierra Infinity exterior ballistics program and found this was not a stellar long-range round. At 500 yards, the Henry's bullet was plunging 486 inches below point of aim—that's 20 feet. Even at 200 yards (using a 100-yard zero), a Western Sharpshooter had to hold his Henry sight 2 feet over his opponent's head to hit him squarely in the chest.

But this rifle wasn't about long-range shooting; it was about firepower, and here the handy Henry had it in droves. With its 16 rounds in the tubular magazine and a 17th in the chamber, Birge's Sharpshooters found the Henry an ideal skirmisher's weapon, giving them a

Though unlikely to fire 60 shots per minute, the Henry lever-action rifle nonetheless was a terror against Confederates armed with single-shots.

tremendous advantage for short- to medium-range fights against enemy soldiers armed with single-shot muzzleloaders. So confident was the manufacturer that Henry ads declared, "A Resolute Man, armed with one of these Rifles, particularly if on horseback, CANNOT BE CAPTURED." The company claimed a firing rate of "sixty shots per minute," but in actual use, especially considering reloading, I'd put the rate more realistically at 32 rounds per minute.

Not only was this a decisive firepower advantage, but the men behind those rifles—Birge's Western Sharpshooters—had the marksmanship skills and combat experience to make each of those shots count. Such men, engaging a force at 200 yards or closer, could create a virtual wall of lead.

The Henry lever-action did not long survive the Civil War. Soon afterward, Benjamin Henry's rifle company was acquired by Oliver Winchester, who improved the design by putting a loading port in the receiver and adding a wooden forearm to protect the shooter's hand from the hot barrel—the Model 1866 Winchester was born and later the Model 1873, "the Gun That Won the West."

CHAPTER FIVE

Sharpshooter Tactics and Techniques

Whether Confederate or Union—Rebel or Yankee—there were great similarities in how Civil War sharpshooters operated and fought. On both sides, sharpshooter units most often were regarded as detachments to be parceled out or split up in direct support of a large unit or spread along a wide front. Many official accounts cite, for instance, "a detachment of Berdan's Sharpshooters, from Whipple's division, accompanied each regiment." Frequently, sharpshooters were dispatched as companies of about 50 to 75 men, who operated in support of a particular regiment. Once under that regiment's control, they were further divided to fit the terrain and the supported unit's mission, even sometimes maneuvering as independent four-man squads.

Both Yankee and Rebel sharpshooters operated as four-man squads.

Tree positions offered good long-range observation and fields of fire, as in this classic Winslow Homer portrayal.

Rarely did sharpshooters camouflage themselves. Here Confederate sharpshooters attempt to conceal themselves in pine boughs.

And here was quite a similarity: both Confederate and Union sharpshooters were organized as four-man squads. This achieved a good balance of firepower and mutual support while keeping their numbers small for concealment and stealthy movement. The major exception was the case of true sniper missions, performed by specially selected sharpshooters armed with telescope rifles or Whitworths. These men maneuvered alone or perhaps with a teammate and operated with tremendous latitude. In Hardee's Confederate brigade, the sharpshooter commander was "given only such orders as were so general in their nature that a large discretion was allowed him." The same was true of a Union sharpshooter with a telescope rifle, "considered an independent character, used only for special service, with the privilege of going to any part of the line where in his own judgment he could do the most good."

Sharpshooters seldom employed special camouflage. Largely this was a matter of personal choice, with John West, a Confederate sharpshooter, recalling that he and his comrades, when concealed in trees, would "pin leaves all over our clothes to keep their color from betraying us."

Cognizant that a heavy rucksack made stealthy movement difficult, Berdan Sharpshooters carried the lightest possible load. The average knapsack, one veteran estimated, weighed 15 pounds, with 40 rounds of ammunition carried in his cartridge case and another 20 on his back. Add to this, of course, his canteen, rifle, and a few pieces of assorted gear, for a grand total of about 40 pounds.

SHARPSHOOTER MISSIONS

The most commonly assigned sharpshooter mission was skirmishing: moving in advance of a larger unit or on its flanks, both as early warning of enemy actions and to "feel out" the enemy's location, size, and activity. While skirmishing, sharpshooters spread out about five paces apart, depending on terrain and foliage, staying close enough to see and signal each other. Usually, this line of skirmishers was about 500 yards forward of the main body, which most often was a regiment.

Distinct from their Northern brothers, Confederate skirmishers also saw their role as an elite assault force "to crush the outer lines and admit our columns to the inner lines and strongholds of the enemy," according to Major William Dunlop, a sharpshooter commander. "And when the opposing armies met upon the field it was [the sharpshooters'] duty to open and bring on the fight, or to stand like ushers on the vestibule of battle and welcome our friends in blue whenever they choose to visit our lines."

Some sharpshooters were called on to scout—the Civil War version of long-range reconnaissance—as two-man teams. The renowned Georgia sharpshooter Berry Benson and his partner, Madison F.

An entire Union regiment practices "battle drill," its sharpshooters (prone) acting as skirmishers to "feel" for the enemy.

A major sharpshooter mission was to dominate the area between the lines with their fire.

Operating as long-range scouts, sharpshooter teams sometimes went deep behind enemy lines.

With great stealth, sharpshooters were sometimes called on to infiltrate enemy lines.

Hawthorn, ran several such hazardous intelligence-gathering missions during the Battles of Spotsylvania and the Wilderness, reporting back directly to General Robert E. Lee. On one occasion they penetrated a Union encampment, obtained important information, and then escaped by stealing a general's horse. The second time Benson attempted that trick, however, he found himself in a Union POW camp.

Other missions could be multifaceted. For example, for one group of Rebel sharpshooters:

> "The general plan was to work themselves at night between the lines, reconnoiter, fix upon a rallying base, and then cover the front of the army, and keep lookout for opportunities to kill off pickets, men who exposed themselves along the line of Federal breast-works, and officers who came in view beyond while directing the operations of their troops. A particular object was to note the position of [artillery] batteries, and take post so as to pick off the gunners through the embrasures."

Using sharpshooters, relentless pressure could be applied on an enemy unit between major battles, lowering morale and denying the enemy rest when he most needed it. For instance, during the Atlanta Campaign, the 33rd Indiana Volunteers, although not in direct contact and simply digging in, suffered unending casualties from hidden Confederate sharpshooters. On Thursday 23 June 1864, the regimental adjutant noted, "Foxworthy, Company H, and Rourke, Company F, severely wounded by sharpshooters." The next day it was "Edwards, Company G, killed, and Farr, Company H, wounded by sharpshooters." And the following day, again, there was "heavy sharpshooting" with "Francis, Company C, badly wounded in the neck." Multiply this attrition by an army's entire front, and these became significant casualties.

Union sharpshooters operated similarly, using their long-range fire to deny Rebel soldiers from observing their positions. Reported the *Richmond Enquirer* in an 1862 article:

> "Here the enemy has been for some time industriously at work, defending their operations against observation by a line of sharpshooters. Several of our men, endeavoring to ascertain what is going on in this sequestered vale, have fallen victims to the rifle shots of the hidden foe."

Due to their sophisticated stalking skills, sharpshooters sometimes were called on for infiltration missions. When Union soldiers in a well-fortified house 100 yards forward of their lines placed effective fire into Confederate positions, an entire company of Rebel sharpshooters was given the mission of eliminating them. Instead of a daylight assault or protracted shooting duel, the Rebs waited for darkness, slipped across the lines, and—in a display of finesse worthy of Sun Tzu, the ancient Chinese strategist—"completely surrounded and quietly captured the entire force consisting of fourteen men without firing a gun, and returned to our lines before daylight."

FIRING POSITIONS

While in the defense or between major battles, sharpshooters often occupied rifle pits (that is, concealed trenches or foxholes between opposing lines) from which they could observe and engage the enemy. In the Confederate Orphan Brigade, the rule was never to place a sharpshooter rifle pit closer than 1/4 mile of the enemy to limit the effectiveness of counterfire. Both Union and Confederate sharpshooters made it a point to dig their rifle pits in darkness, use them during the day,

This Confederate sharpshooter, armed with a Whitworth, wisely uses a tree trunk for ballistic protection.

Rarely could two sharpshooters occupy a single tree, but in this case they were luring Union scouts.

Angry Officers

At the Battle of Fort Donelson, a body of keen-eyed Birge's Western Sharpshooters were knocking down Confederate soldiers all along the works. In a forward position, the legendary Confederate cavalry commander, General Nathan Bedford Forrest, grew angry at the one-sided casualties. Detecting a Birge Sharpshooter in a tree, he borrowed a soldier's Maynard rifle "and rather foolishly exposing himself . . . fired at the unfortunate soldier, who tumbled headlong to the ground." Forrest, who lived a charmed life, had once again demonstrated the daring for which he was famous.

Unlike General Nathan Bedford Forrest, who shot a Union sharpshooter at Fort Donelson, officers who fired at sharpshooters typically lost such contests.

Other angry officers who personally fired at sharpshooters were not so fortunate. Captain Edward Acton, 5th New Jersey Volunteer Infantry, at the Second Battle of Bull Run, grew "irritated" by Confederate sharphooters wounding his men. Borrowing a rifle, Acton sought out, found, and killed a Rebel marksman. However, he had revealed his position, and thus, while reloading, another Confederate sharpshooter shot him. In less than an hour he expired.

Lieutenant Colonel Victor De Monteil, executive officer of the 53rd New York Regiment, grabbed a rifle to join other men exchanging fire with sharpshooters during a landing in North Carolina. Lieutenant Colonel De Monteil "was coolly loading, firing and watching the effect of each shot," one account states. And that's when he was killed.

At sea it was equally hazardous for naval officers to do battle with sharpshooters. Acting Ensign Henry Jackson, U.S. Navy, in 1864 observed a Confederate flag flying from a captured Union ship. Emotionally moved, the young ensign borrowed a rifle to shoot down the enemy colors and was himself shot dead by a Rebel sharpshooter.

Confederate Navy Captain Franklin Buchanan, a veteran of nearly 50 years' service and the founding commandant of the U.S. Naval Academy, in 1862 commanded the famous ironclad CSS *Virginia*. It was Captain Buchanan who won history's first engagement by an ironclad, sinking three wooden Union ships and three small steamers at Hampton Roads, Virginia. At the end of that fight, angry with some plinking by Union sharpshooters, Buchanan left behind the armor protection of his iron hull to go "topside to return fire with a Sharps carbine." Of course the sharpshooters prevailed, seriously wounding Captain Buchanan. But his pain was doubled, for the very next day one of the most pivotal naval engagements of all history occurred: the "battle of the ironclads," CSS *Virginia* versus the USS *Monitor*. And Buchanan could only watch from afar, having relinquished command to obtain medical treatment.

and then pull back to friendly lines after dusk. When it was necessary to build and occupy a rifle pit in daylight, according to Union sharpshooter James Conrad Peters, he and his cohorts would crawl "about a half a mile on our hands and knees with shovels" and then scrape out a shallow recess to lie within, pushing dirt to the front for ballistic protection. Operating thusly, the Sharps rifle–armed Berdan Sharpshooters had a significant advantage: being able to reload their breechloaders while prone. Doing likewise with a muzzleloader was a clumsy, tedious affair for Confederate sharpshooters and considerably reduced their rate of fire.

At the 1864 Battle of the Wilderness, a Confederate officer reported, "The Federal sharpshooters here taught us a lesson, by firing obliquely up and down the line, away to the left or right, instead of straight ahead." This allowed Union marksmen to hit far-away Rebel soldiers taking cover behind trees, while the Federals could not be hit by nearby enemy soldiers firing directly from their front. A brilliant tactic, it would be reborn in the trenches of World War I.

When fighting from hillcrests or behind dirt ridges, Berdan Sharpshooters improvised loopholes "by forcing sharpened stakes through the bank of earth," after which "woe to that unfortunate rebel who exposed even a small portion of his figure within the circumscribed range of their vision."

Firing positions in trees were quite popular because they offered observation and fields of fire superior to ground level. Ideally, the sharpshooter sat on a wide branch for a degree of comfort and stability, with another branch at shoulder height to support his rifle. His body was close to the trunk for frontal protection, and, if he was lucky, the leaves or pine boughs obscured the puff of his gunpowder. The downsides were reloading while perched on a branch and the hazard of getting down if he was spotted, along with the difficulty of aiming when wind swayed the tree. The most effective tree position was well back in a grove of trees, to make him more difficult to detect.

On occasion, special firing positions were constructed for sharpshooters, most often during sieges such as Vicksburg and Petersburg. At Sullivan's Island, South Carolina, for example, the U.S. Army Corps of Engineers constructed a special tower—reminiscent of the Maham Towers of the Revolutionary War—for advantageous firing by sharpshooters.

TECHNIQUES OF FIRE

Unlike conventional infantry, Civil War sharpshooters did not await an officer's command, "Commence firing!" Whether skirmishing, in rifle pits, atop trees, or on picket duty, they normally used their own judgment when circumstances required them to open fire. As accomplished marksmen, they had the shooting experience and as sharpshooters the tactical leeway to seek support for their rifle and exploit cover against enemy counterfire; this ensured both that they hit what they were aiming at and that hostile return fire would not hit them.

For long-range shooting—especially using telescope rifles or Whitworths—they sought the steadiest support available, whether a horse carcass, a hay bale, or a tripod. Tripod firing was instructed to Confederate sharpshooters in the spring of 1864, as recounted in Major Dunlop's book, *Lee's Sharpshooters*. So similar was this to the method taught at the British Hythe School of Musketry—placing a sandbag at the apex of three 6-foot poles lashed together—that I suspect they drew on Hythe materials to prepare the course.

Sharpshooters on both sides learned all sorts of tricks and sneaky techniques. For example, they perfected a special kind of precision volley fire, with each man aiming at a target for a surprise effect or to ensure a hit at great distance or in gusty winds. Though it looked like a volley, actually this was

Shooting the Sharpshooter Who Killed Colonel Starnes

Colonel James W. Starnes, commander of the 4th Tennessee Cavalry Regiment, was said to have "no fault, unless it was the constant rash exposure of himself to danger." On 30 June 1863, near Tullahoma, Tennessee, as Captain W.A. Hubbard advanced with skirmishers into heavy Union fire, he found Colonel Starnes approaching. Hubbard begged his "beloved commander" to retire to the relative safety of the main line. Starnes thanked him for his concern "but, as usual, remained at the front."

Momentarily, a Union sharpshooter spotted the regimental commander. One well-aimed shot ended Colonel Starnes' life. "Thus fell this worthy physician, brave soldier and noble man, in the prime of life and on the threshold of a great career," wrote an admirer.

The anonymous Union sharpshooter may have realized he'd shot an important officer—but we'll never know his thoughts. For a Confederate sharpshooter named Jackson, from Ashland, Tennessee, happened upon the scene and spotted the concealed sharpshooter's puff of smoke, high in a tree. Reported a witness, Jackson "picked his way cautiously . . . until he had a safe range upon the Federal, and at the crack of his gun the man fell from the tree like a squirrel before the rifle of a trained hunter."

Killed by a Union sharpshooter, Colonel James W. Starnes had his death avenged moments later by a Confederate sharpshooter.

Support was crucial to well-aimed fire, even if it was a horse carcass.

a "simultaneous engagement," with a group of fine marksmen letting loose at the same instant. This is how Virginia sharpshooters killed Union Brigadier General James A. Mulligan on 26 July 1864, despite the great range. Realizing that there was only about a 30 percent chance of hitting him, seven marksmen all took careful aim and then fired simultaneously—and afterward regretted it, for Mulligan had treated Southern prisoners well and was deeply respected.

Other Confederate sharpshooters employed a series of simultaneous engagements to win the day at the Battle of Ream's Station, Virginia, on 24 August 1864. Facing a numerically superior Union force, a battalion of Rebel sharpshooters fell back to good cover at a hillcrest 600 yards away and planned their response. Quoting their commander:

> "Here, deliberately but without malice, planning the destruction of their enemies, the sharpshooters carefully estimated the distance between the lines, the depression of the ground where the enemy lay, the course the ball would take in its trajectory flight, and the exact point where it would cut the line of fire; then adjusting their sights accordingly, they entered upon the work at hand."

At his command, the entire battalion rose above the hillcrest, took quick aim at Union soldiers exposed all along the facing wood line, and "delivered a volley then dropped back down to load." Continuing this deadly routine "for five mortal hours [we] swept the Union breastworks with a perfect sheet of lead . . . and with unerring aim proceeded to split the scalp of every mother's son that dared to lift his head above the breastworks." Runners brought forward additional ammunition, allowing the Rebel marksmen to fire an astonishing 160 aimed rounds apiece. Eventually the Union force "fled through the woods in the wildest confusion."

To be sure, the Confederates had no monopoly on clever techniques. An officer of the 20th Ohio Infantry Regiment recalled how his sharpshooters sometimes made "a tremendous shout, and when the enemy bob up to see what is going on they give them a telling volley, and then roll over and kick their heels up in the air in great joy."

Some tricks were pure improvisations. Hearing Union troops digging in total darkness 100 yards away, a South Carolina sharpshooter officer, Lieutenant J.D. McConnell, knew there was little hope of hitting them—then a thought struck him. He ordered one company, from the safety of a trench, to fire blindly toward the Union troops. Sure enough, the whole Union line returned fire—which perfectly illuminated them for another company of South Carolinians, rifles cocked and ready at their shoulders, to fire with telling effect. "We killed five," McConnell reported, "all in [colorful] Zouave uniform."

ENGAGING ENEMY ARTILLERY

There was no sharpshooter mission more demanding—and so hazardous when done improperly—than engaging artillery crews. Unlike the 20th century, when artillery units used forward observers and radios to engage distant targets the gunners could not see, artillery pieces of the 19th century had to employ "direct fire," meaning the gun crews personally eyeballed their targets. And if a Civil War artillery crew could see their targets, they, too, could be seen and engaged.

Positioning himself further than 400 yards from an enemy cannon, the sharpshooter knew he was beyond the effective range of its canister round, also called "grapeshot" since it spewed a bucketful of grape-size lead balls. Thus, when firing from 500 or more yards—still within the accurate range of his rifle—a sharpshooter could make life hell for loaders and gunners, who had to show themselves to operate their guns. Not only did an artilleryman have to load at the bore, but another crewman first had to swab it with water to extinguish embers from the previous round and ram down a powder sack. Further, each time the gun shifted targets, a gunner had to look down a brass sight placed at the rear of the barrel.

According to one Confederate officer:

> "Ordinarily, if these sharpshooters could place themselves in sight of the enemy's can-nons, with fair cover, and within a quarter to half mile, it was almost certain death or disabling for a Federal soldier to swab or load after discharge, as he could not protect himself when his gun was in position."

CSA Brigadier General W.L. Cabell, Commanding Northwest Arkansas, had to report to his higher headquarters:

> "I regret to say I lost a good many [artillery] horses. The enemy's sharpshooters killed a good many with their long-range guns. . . . Had I had 500 long-range [rifles] with good cartridges, I could have taken the place in an hour. As it was, I could not advance my battery, as I had nothing to cover them with, as the enemy's [sharpshooter] guns were equal in range to the artillery."

Cannon crews were especially vulnerable to sharpshooters while unlimbering and positioning guns because at that moment, rapid emplacement was usually thought more important than seeking cover from enemy fire. While positioning his guns during the Atlanta Campaign, Lieutenant James Hurst of the 2nd Missouri Artillery Regiment "was killed by a sharpshooter." At Chickamauga, Union

Even behind thick cover, gun crews still had to expose themselves to load and aim their cannons.

Major James Hampson was shot dead by a sharpshooter while positioning artillery. Lieutenant Orrin B. Carpenter of the 9th New York Heavy Artillery similarly was shot dead while aligning guns at the Battle of Cedar Creek. This happened so frequently that it almost became an everyday hazard, an unending cost of battle.

In many cases, sharpshooters merely suppressing artillery was acceptable—that is, placing such hazardous fire that the crews backed away from their guns. When Colonel Giles Smith of the 8th Missouri ordered his sharpshooters forward, "they advanced to within 100 yards of the guns, which they effectually silenced, not only picking off every gunner who showed himself above the works, but killing every horse belonging to the artillery."

While manning their guns, artillery crews were particularly vulnerable to sharpshooter fire.

"Whenever a gunner exposed himself in the least," a *New York Herald* correspondent wrote from a Virginia battlefield, "he found he immediately became the target for innumerable concealed and unerring marksmen. Flesh and blood could not face the ordeal, and serving these guns was temporarily abandoned."

At the Battle of Spotsylvania, the Berdan Sharpshooters took on three Confederate artillery bat-

Artillery Sharpshooters

Artillerymen did not usually refer to themselves as sharpshooters, but in an engagement on 19 November 1863, a gun crew from Battery E, 2nd U.S. Artillery, proved themselves truly worthy of the title.

That day, during fighting in Knoxville, Tennessee, Rebel sharpshooters had occupied General James Longstreet's former headquarters in a stately home known as Bleak House. Taking positions in the house's prominent turret, the Whitworth-armed marksmen had a considerable field of fire, deep into Union lines. Spotting a distinct figure, undoubtedly a senior officer, one sharpshooter took careful aim—and got his man.

The shock could not have been worse to Union forces fighting at Knoxville. Mortally wounded from one well-aimed shot was their division commander, Major General William Price Sanders.

Not far from where Major General Sanders fell stood Fort Loudon, where Lieutenant Samuel Benjamin commanded the Union artillery battery. Learning that the fatal shot had come from the Bleak House's distant turret—fully 2,500 yards away—Lieutenant Benjamin took especial care in calculating the range, adjusting one gun's elevation, even taking into account the effect of the wind. Then he fired.

It was perfect. The parrot gun's projectile impacted directly on the turret, killing three sharpshooters and forcing the rest to flee. Lieutenant Benjamin's was quite likely the most accurate deliberate artillery shot of the war.

And, if you're interested, the stately Bleak House still exists. Open to the public for meetings and receptions, its restored turret displays a pencil drawing of the sharpshooters who died there, one of whom is buried on the grounds.

When a Rebel sharpshooter killed Major General William Price Sanders, an extreme-range artillery shot avenged his death.

teries. "They would try to load their pieces by reaching up under the muzzle," wrote a sharpshooter, "but the boys could send a Sharps rifle ball so completely in the muzzles of their cannon at this distance that they could not load."

Occasionally, sharpshooter fire proved so totally overwhelming that the guns were completely abandoned. At Bristoe Station, Virginia, on 14 October 1863, the 1st Company of Andrews Sharpshooters did not merely drive off the gun crews, but rushed forward and captured the guns. "I think they deserve the highest praise for the well timed audacity of the scheme," wrote Union Major Henry Abbott. But for one damaged cannon, all saw further service in Union batteries.

Instead of capturing it, other sharpshooters demonstrated that they could actually destroy an enemy gun with precision fire. During the Yorktown siege, Lieutenant Martin V. Bronson of Berdan's Sharpshooters announced that a heavy Confederate gun dubbed "Petersburg" would blow up if precisely placed shots could throw sand and gravel down its bore. A former artilleryman, Lieutenant Bronson and several sharpshooters fired numerous rounds into sandbags at the gun's muzzle, splashing

Countering Confederate artillery, Berdan Sharpshooters pick off enemy gun crews.

Confederate artillerymen lie dead about their battery. Killing or suppressing gun crews was a primary mission for sharpshooters.

The 10th Massachusetts battery commander, Captain J. Henry Sleeper (standing, center), whose artillerymen were riddled with sharpshooter fire.

abrasive sand down the barrel. Sure enough, when the gun fired its thirteenth round, it blew up. This is, however, the only instance I've come across where this technique succeeded.

At times these artillery-sharpshooter engagements became all-out duels. Confederate sharpshooters firing from a house at Manassas, Virginia, shot down so many horses that a Union battery could not move and then began knocking down the crews—who turned their undivided attention and their guns toward the house. In quick salvos, their six cannons literally blew the house to bits, along with anything that was inside.

Some artillery batteries integrated the fire of supporting sharpshooters for maximum effectiveness. Recalled a Union artillery officer:

> "We had the advantage of position
> having posted our battery so it
> would sweep the road for nearly a
> mile. We hid our sharpshooters
> also in the edge of the swamp and
> when the [Rebel] battery would
> reply to our's, those keen eyed
> marksmen would pick off their
> artillerymen, so that our battery
> had much the best of the fight."

In that case artillerymen appreciated the support of sharpshooters, but this was not always true. On 24 June 1864 near Petersburg, Berdan Sharpshooter James Ragin was requested to support an artillery battery, its commander desiring "to witness Ragin's skill in long-range shooting." The keen-eyed Ragin obligingly let loose a series of deadly shots from his 34-pound telescope rifle into a distant Confederate battery—which then poured shells on the Union artillery position. "Thereupon in a profane and excited manner," the account finishes, the artillery officer "ordered Ragin away."

Concentrated sharpshooter fire, in some situations, tore artillery batteries quickly to shreds. At Ream's Station, Virginia, the 10th Massachusetts Battery, "one of the best in the service," according to *Harper's Weekly*, suffered such a fate. Commanded by Captain J. Henry Sleeper, a prominent Bostonian, the battery was setting up when Confederate marksmen from McGowan's Sharpshooters took aim from 300 yards away. First to fall was Hosea O. Barnes, on the number-three gun. Next, Captain Sleeper was shot through the arm, and Lieutenant H.H. Granger assumed command. Then, a teamster, John Goodwin, took a round through the shoulder. Charles Mason, a driver on the number-one gun, and Samuel H. Foster, another driver, were both shot in the head. William Rawson was shot in the foot, and Lieutenant Granger had his pistol shot out of his hands. Then Lieutenants Adams and Smith were mortally shot. Of the battery's 24 horses, only two were still standing, and one caisson was exploded by incoming fire.

Imagine, then, the continuing losses, the ever-present dangers artillerymen felt from sharpshooters—and how readily they would return the compliment when given the chance. That's what happened at the 1862 Battle of Frayser's Farm, where General James Longstreet "sent orders for [Brigadier General Micah] Jenkins to silence [a] battery" that was firing into his position. What Longstreet intended was that Jenkins' "sharp-shooters would be pushed forward till they could pick off the gunners, thus ridding us of that annoyance." Unfortunately for the Palmetto Sharpshooters, that is not how Colonel Jenkins interpreted it.

Instead of placing precision rifle fire on the Union guns, Jenkins had the whole battalion rush the guns across open ground. The air singing with grapeshot, the Palmetto Sharpshooters charged through volley after volley of canister rounds. Yes, they did capture six guns. But behind them strewn across the field was a ghastly sight; the Palmetto Sharpshooters had lost 67 percent of its men, killed and wounded—an unnecessary catastrophe, thought General Longstreet, who blamed the tragic affair on Jenkins.

COUNTERING SHARPSHOOTERS

As demonstrated in Jenkins' charge, one of the most effective Civil War counter-sharpshooter weapons was an artillery piece, especially when firing canister rounds packed with inch-wide lead

His gun crews shot or forced to cover by Berdan's Sharpshooters, a Rebel artillery captain forces slaves at gunpoint to man an artillery piece.

This mantelet shield protected Rebel gun crews at Petersburg from Union sharpshooters—except when they had to load or swab the bore.

This dirt-filled wicker cylinder "sap roller," weighing up to a ton, protected engineers from sharpshooter fire while they were digging trenches.

shot. Like a gigantic shotgun, hundreds of these grape-sized projectiles riddled a swath 25 yards wide, to a distance of 400 yards. Beyond that range, solid or explosive shells had to be fired with considerable accuracy to hit a target as small as an individual sharpshooter. Despite this, Rebel sharpshooter John West learned that artillerymen "would turn their guns upon a sharpshooter as quick as they would upon a battery."

Keen to the danger of canister rounds, most sharpshooters wisely fired from farther than 400 yards, but some gun crews had the skill to fire solid rounds accurately at a considerable distance. Confederate artilleryman James M. Dancy recorded in his journal what happened when a Federal sharpshooter began placing effective fire on his crew:

> "A sharpshooter in a tall cypress got the range of Lieut. Hines' gun and with a globe-sighted rifle fired three shots. One struck the axle; one struck the face of the gun; the third shattered the left arm of the gunner, George Griffin. Our gun sergeant with his glass had located this sharpshooter by the puffs of smoke from a large cypress tree about a quarter of a mile away . . . about fifty feet from the ground. He trained our gun, loaded with a twelve-pound solid shot. After the report, no more shots were fired. . . . Our solid shot had passed through the sharpshooter's body, cutting it nearly in two."

Oftentimes it was not just one cannon returning fire. "Just as soon as we'd see one of those little puffs

Drawing Fire

Civil War sharpshooters inflicted considerable losses wherever they appeared. In many cases, however, the targeting of these casualties was facilitated by the target's own conspicuous action or bold uniform—they were practically "self-targeted."

Captain Joseph Abbott of the 7th New Jersey Volunteer Infantry, for example, "was shot in the forehead and instantly killed while waving his sword for encouragement" at the Second Battle of Bull Run. Abbott's courageous display was admirable—but, equally, that gesture drew the attention of sharpshooters. As Stonewall Jackson had logically remarked after learning one of his Rebel sharpshooters had shot an especially courageous Union officer, "I want the brave officers of the enemy killed off. Their death insures our success."

It wasn't only captains who drew fire by their gestures. At Fort Donelson, CSA Lieutenant Colonel Alfred Robb rode his white horse among his men, cheering them and waving his arm—and then a Union sharpshooter shot him dead. The commander of the Union's 3rd Division at the Second Battle of Kernstown, Brigadier General James Mulligan, too, rode among his soldiers, halted and raised up on his saddle to cheer—and that's when a well-timed distant volley, a simultaneous engagement by seven Rebel sharpshooters, struck him down. "He probably would not have been killed," wrote a veteran of the action, "but for the persistency of his color guard in waving a flag" beside him. They may as well have raised a sign, "Shoot here!"

Another senior officer who boldly posed beside his unit colors was Colonel Leander Stem of the 101st Ohio Infantry. When his regiment began to waiver at the Battle of Stones River, he shouted to his men, "Stand by the flag now, for the good old State of Ohio." Instantly he fell, mortally wounded.

A distinguished upbringing provided no protection from sharpshooter fire. Theodore Winthrop, a direct descendant of Massachusetts' first governor, a Yale graduate, and a successful author, was on the staff of Union Major General Benjamin Butler. On 10 June 1861, watching Rebel forces rout Butler's troops, Winthrop ran among the fleeing soldiers, jumped on a log, and shouted, "One more charge and the day is ours!" He'd hardly spoken the last word when a sharpshooter's bullet killed him, "a meaningless casualty of a day already lost."

Conspicuous clothing—plumed hats, for instance—also drew sharp-

Some officers believed their conspicuous actions and gaudy uniforms inspired their troops, but frequently this also drew sharpshooter fire.

Expressing pride, early in the war some units wore colorful uniforms, like the checkered shirt of this 4th Michigan Regiment private. Later they knew better.

A useful sharpshooter aiming point: the bright brass shield on Union infantrymen's chest cross-strap.

By midwar, the brass shield "aiming point" had been eliminated.

shooter fire. Colonel Gilbert Elliot, commanding the 102nd New York Volunteers, went forward at Lookout Mountain to lead his regimental skirmishers—wearing a bright red cape. One unit history notes, "He wore a full uniform with a red-lined cape . . . making a conspicuous mark, and he was the first man hit in the engagement."

Such questionable judgment was not a Yankee monopoly. Major Abner Carmichael, executive officer of the 26th North Carolina, a man of unquestionable courage, was standing beside his regimental commander when "a bullet entered his mouth and exited the back of his neck," killing him. As that unit's history observes, "It was possible that the Federal [sharpshooter] who fired this shot saw a small Confederate flag, three by four inches in size, that was mounted on a miniature staff attached to Carmichael's cap."

Depending on the range, indeed, a sharpshooter's telescope may have honed in on that display of patriotism—or, as he saw it, a target indicator.

Less ostentatious actions could draw sharpshooter fire, too. In direct view of the enemy lines at Yorktown, Union Lieutenant Colonel Francis W. Palfrey "was crouching down examining the enemy's works with a glass, when a ball, fired from a rifle pit by a Rebel sharpshooter, struck his knee and shattered the bones down to the middle of the calf." Lieutenant Colonel Palfrey survived, but surgeons had to amputate his leg.

Saluting within view of the enemy could be dangerous, too. At the Battle of Kennesaw Mountain, Major General M.D. Leggett was walking among the men of the 50th Ohio when Captain William Neal spotted his division commander. Captain Neal snapped to attention, saluted—and was struck dead by a sharpshooter's bullet that passed through his body and killed a horse. Major General Leggett, the likely target, was not injured.

Understandably, as the effectiveness of sharpshooting grew, there were attempts to reduce the "signature" or conspicuousness of uniforms. Early in the war, the cross-strap on Union infantrymen's chests had a bright brass shield at its center, which soon became a useful aiming point for long-range shooting. The decorative shield was eliminated, leaving only the plain strap. So many Union officers were being shot that General James Rosecrans' Army of the Cumberland issued General Order No. 174 on 25 July 1863. "In order to prevent the disorganization of the army, its officers being picked off by the enemy's sharpshooters," the order began, and then detailed changes in displays of rank to make officers more difficult to distinguish. During the trying days of the Petersburg siege, when Union soldiers fell night and day to Confederate sharpshooter fire, the 9th Corps banned bright brass fixtures on cartridge cases and belts.

All such measures, however, had only a limited effect.

of smoke," recalled a Confederate veteran, "the entire battery would rain shot and shell into that tree, and we'd make it so hot for the sharpshooter that he'd either tumble or crawl out, dead or alive."

The sharpshooter frequently did not realize until too late that he'd been targeted by artillery. At the Battle of Jones Farm in July 1864, a treetop Union telescope rifle sharpshooter was placing deadly fire among a North Carolina regiment. When spotted almost a mile away, Rebel officers realized "there was not a small arm in the Division that would carry effectively one-fourth that distance." But what the sharpshooter didn't know was that McGregor's Artillery Battery was hidden in the adjacent woods. "McGregor carefully measured the distance," explained a North Carolina officer, "trained one of his six-pound guns upon the object, loaded with a shell with fuse cut nicely and sighted by his most skillful gunner, exploded the shell at the sharpshooter's feet." That was the end of that.

The more effective the sharpshooter, the more rounds he received in counterfire. At Cold Harbor on 6 June 1864, a Confederate battery fired salvo after salvo at Berdan Sharpshooter Wyman C. White, expending "as much as fifty shots slam bang into the place where I had been firing." Fortunately for White, he was able to get below ground.

Sometimes, despite the apparent superiority of firepower, these exchanges backfired for the cannoneers. Edward S. Small, a New Hampshire man, and a handful of comrades were plinking away at Confederate positions on Chickahominy Creek when a Rebel artillery battery arrived to do them in. As the Confederate artillerymen unlimbered their guns, the Yankee sharpshooters poured fire on them, killing several horses and knocking down a number of men, with one lucky shot smacking into an ammunition chest, setting off a secondary explosion. The surviving artillerymen fled for their lives.

Contrary to the South's image of chivalry, Union sharpshooters drove one desperate Confederate artillery officer to a seedy display of cowardice. After precision fire had knocked down a number of his crews, making it impossible to reload their guns, the Rebel captain drew his pistol and forced slaves to load a cannon. The terror on their faces was captured in an illustration published by *Harper's Weekly*, and apparently brought enough shame that the despicable countertactic was not used again.

A more frequently encountered defensive measure was placing mantelets before artillery pieces to deflect or absorb sharpshooter fire. These shields, made of iron or even thick-woven rope (see page 91), allowed the crew to aim and fire, but it was still hazardous to swab and load.

All sorts of other techniques and devices were employed to minimize the effectiveness of sharpshooter fire. While digging trenches, engineers rolled before them enormous "sap rollers"—dirt-packed, basketlike woven cylinders weighing almost a ton. Impervious even to Whitworth slugs, this mobile cover

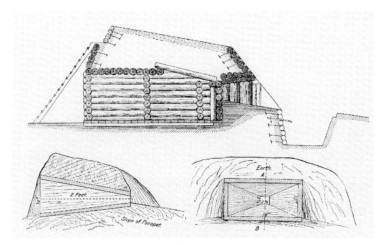

Union engineers prefabricated this special bunker to withstand Confederate Whitworth sharpshooter fire at Fort Fisher, North Carolina.

The "Soldier's Bullet Proof Vest" was heavily advertised in newspapers, but it did not live up to its claims. (Original art by Tami Anderson.)

allowed engineers to safely dig trenches and fighting positions. Barricades were constructed from whatever was available—logs, rocks, even cotton bales. As quickly as fire erupted, many wizened infantrymen began stacking rocks for cover, considerable lengths of which are still visible at Gettysburg today.

To deny sharpshooters cover or concealment along the Potomac shore—and thereby make for safer water travel—the Union Army burned large stretches of its western bank. More directly, torching buildings was a way of flushing or killing sharpshooters inside. In Knoxville, Tennessee, on 20 November 1863, Irwin Shepard, Andrew J. Kelley, and John Falconer earned Medals of Honor for having been the "burning party" of the 17th Michigan Infantry sent "to destroy buildings behind the enemy's lines from which sharpshooters had been firing."

Whitworth sharpshooter fire was so deadly at Fort Fisher, North Carolina, that a Union engineer, a Captain King, mass-produced a special, one-man log bunker. "And where there was much sharpshooting," a report explains, "the orifice [firing port] was still further reduced by a plate of thin boiler iron eight or ten inches square, with a hole in the center but little larger than the barrel of a musket."

A more personal kind of cover—body armor—was commercially manufactured in New York and sold through ads in major newspapers. In ads proclaiming "it will save thousands," the "Soldier's Bullet Proof Vest" was purported to stop pistol bullets at 10 paces and rifle bullets at 40 rods (220 yards). One member of Berdan's Sharpshooters, known by the nickname "Snap Shot," wore such a vest but eventually threw it away, complaining, "I have carried that weighty nuisance long enough." How well did it work? Dr. J.V. Harris, a Confederate officer, found one at Shiloh that, he reported, "had a bullet hole through it . . . just over the position of the heart." A specimen found on the Gettysburg battlefield is displayed today at the museum there.

In lieu of body armor, there were many ways to safely respond to sharpshooter fire. The simplest and most obvious—if you survived the sharpshooter's first shot—was simply to get out of his line of fire. It easily took a minute or more to reload a Whitworth or telescope rifle, especially if the hidden rifleman was perched in a treetop, quite enough time to find a better place to be.

There are many accounts of would-be victims actually dodging the sharpshooter's round, virtually leaping out of its way like something in the *Matrix* movies. This, too, was common sense, *if* you spotted the "puff" of his shot.

Knowing the weight and muzzle velocity of a typical sharpshooter's round, I ran the data through my Sierra ballistic software and found that at 300 yards, you had one second before it reached you, two seconds at 500 yards, and three seconds at 800 yards. That's a lot of time, plenty to see the "puff" and then drop or jump for cover—the key factor being detecting the muzzle blast.

This dodging tactic became sufficiently widespread that sharpshooters sometimes took it into account when planning a shot. At Gettysburg, Union sharpshooters realized that Confederate sharpshooters firing from a house would see the smoke of their muzzles, so they split into two elements. One element fired and, sure enough,

To discover hidden sharpshooters, troops of both sides lured fire with various ruses.

Extreme-Range Shots

Civil War literature abounds with tales of amazing long-distance shots, with some claims exceeding the accuracy and range of sniper weapons 100 years later. How credible are these stories?

Some confusion arises because British engineer Joseph Whitworth applied his hexagonal projectile technology to both a sharpshooter's rifle and a light artillery piece of about 70mm. To distinguish its rifled bore from that of smooth-bore artillery, this, too, was called a "Whitworth rifle" and fired its six-sided shell a mile or more. I think modern readers have sometimes misattributed extreme-range Whitworth artillery hits to the Confederate sharpshooter's rifle of the same name.

Eyewitness claims, too, sometimes challenge logic. Mile-long shots? One mile is 1,760 yards, well beyond the Whitworth sight's maximum elevation, meaning a sharpshooter would have had to "hold" dozens of feet above the target to put a round that far, which is contrary to the precise aim needed to hit a tiny target at great range. And even using a 4x scope, a human silhouette is a mighty tiny speck 1 mile away.

The Whitworth's known accuracy also challenges such performance. The 1857 British Ordnance tests included firing at 1,800 yards—40 yards over a mile—and generated a group radius of 139 inches, meaning a total diameter spread of 278 inches.

This test, I believe, exaggerated the spread due to crosswinds and the relatively low-powered scopes of that era. A more realistic long-range accuracy estimate can be extrapolated from the Whitworth's 100-yard groups—where optics perform well and wind has minimal effect—using a measurement called minutes of angle (MOA). Here's how that works: at 100 yards a Whitworth group measures 1.75 inches, pretty typical for that rifle. That group widens with distance; logically, it will be twice as wide at twice that distance, meaning it will spread to 3.5 inches at 200 yards. Very handily, the angular measurement, MOA, widens at almost exactly the same rate; at 100 yards 1 MOA equals 1 inch, at 200 it's 2 inches, at 500 it's 5 inches, and so on. Thus,

Berdan Sharpshooters fire heavy "telescope rifles" at great range, 1862. (Courtesy of William H. Hastings.)

instead of saying the Whitworth 100-yard group measured 1.75 inches, we can call it 1.75 MOA—and then by simple multiplication calculate this group at 1 mile, or 1,760 yards: 1.75 MOA x 17.6 = 30.8 inches. That's a foot wider than an average man's torso, telling me that even under ideal conditions—the exact range known, no effect from crosswinds, and a world-class marksman—the odds of a first-round hit at a mile are pretty iffy, at best a bit better than 50-50.

Doing the same calculations for a Union telescope rifle, the Morgan James, cuts the 1-mile group in half. This rifle's stubbier Minie ball, however, lacked the Whitworth hexagonal bullet's ballistic efficiency, meaning the Morgan James required even a higher elevation hold and was more susceptible to drift in a crosswind.

All that said, there genuinely were some remarkable extreme-range hits with Civil War sharpshooter rifles—but just keep in mind that in wartime no one records the misses, which, statistically, must have been numerous.

DOCUMENTED EXTREME-RANGE SHOTS

Civil War sharpshooter unit histories did not find it worth commenting on shots of less than 700 yards, which was about the maximum range for the Berdan Sharpshooters' .52-caliber Sharps rifles. The July 1862 skirmish at Orange Court

House was noted in their unit history because their bullets had "trajected over the entire length of a 700-yard field" and Confederate prisoners later verified their effectiveness. During another engagement, two Sharps-armed riflemen fired simultaneously at a Reb soldier some 700 yards away—and both their rounds hit, the wounded man later told his captors.

For firing beyond 700 yards, Berdan marksmen almost exclusively employed their heavy-barreled telescope rifles. And this threshold, too, crossed into the realm of the Confederate Whitworth sharpshooter.

When firing at extreme range, Confederate sharpshooters used a "rest stick," a tall tripod with a sandbag at its apex, a technique learned from the British.

No more knowledgeable or reliable witnesses to a long-range shot could be found than the Berdan Sharpshooters, so I have no doubt that the Confederate bullet that killed Union Major General Amiel Whipple at Chancellorsville actually was fired from a half-mile away—or 880 yards—as they reported. One day earlier, at nearby Hazel Grove, a Confederate officer, Captain Greenlee Davidson, was killed by a sharpshooter firing from 800 yards, demonstrating that the Union telescope rifle, too, was effective.

The Whitworth's deadliness was well known to Union officers, with one colonel realistically noting, "When we were within one-half [880 yards] or three-fourths [1,320 yards] of a mile of the enemy, the effect of their sharp-shooters was terrible."

The colonel's view was correct, with any number of hits at better than a half-mile. During the Gettysburg Campaign, Second Lieutenant Ben Gough, 12th West Virginia Infantry, was cited in an official dispatch as having been "shot by a Rebel sharpshooter at not less than 900 yards distance." Such accuracy was not to be outdone by a Union telescope rifle, however, with Captain Samuel McKittrick, 16th South Carolina, falling to a 900-yard shot on 22 July 1864 outside Atlanta.

Reflecting as much their ingenuity as their accuracy, a handful of Berdan Sharpshooters scored hits with their Sharps rifles at an amazing 1,500 yards—nearly nine-tenths of a mile—at Todd's Tavern, Virginia. This challenge was given them by Lieutenant General Winfield Hancock, who wanted the Confederate observers vacated from a distant signal tower, a mission already attempted and failed by an artillery battery.

Their Sharps' sights maxing out at 1,000 yards, they scratched their heads and then whittled sticks to fashion extensions that further raised their rear sights. Three sharpshooters fired at the distant tower while an officer using binoculars watched the enemy soldiers look down—"Low!" he called. The sharpshooters fired more spotter rounds, and the Rebs looked up—"High!" he called. Now, with the position bracketed, some 23 sharpshooters similarly attached sight extensions and then, firing simultaneously, cleared the tower.

At the receiving end, the lethality of extreme-range Whitworth slugs was well documented. A *New York Herald* reporter with Union troops outside Fort Sumter noted no one had yet been hit by Confederate sharpshooters firing Whitworths at more than three-quarters of a mile, but "the bolts reach [here] with enough velocity to perforate any respectable thick head which they may come in contact with. . . ."

There are several accounts of both Confederate and Union sharpshooters scoring hits at 1 mile, but these appeared in postwar veteran publications, not wartime journals or official reports. Relying on memory 30 years after the events, they must be regarded with some degree of skepticism.

By contrast the greatest Civil War extreme-range shot, which has been repeated far and wide in magazines, in books, and on television, simply never happened. This legendary mile-long shot originally appeared in the 1946 book *Our Rifles* and was attributed to "John Metcalf the 3d," an alleged West Point graduate and phenomenal marksman. Staking out a Union general's tent, the story goes, Metcalf was assisted by an engineer officer to precisely calculate the range, adjust his sights, and so forth, and then finally made his amazing shot. Versions of the story appeared in a 1961 *True* Magazine article and even generated an episode of the General Electric Hour on national television. The problem, explains NRA National Firearms Museum Curator Doug Wickland, is that none of this story checks out. The graduate rosters of West Point do not contain any "John H. Metcalf III," nor do Civil War records include a distinguished sharpshooter of that name.

As a Confederate of such great achievement, he should at least have been mentioned in *The Confederate Veteran*, the magazine published by Southern veterans, but that did not happen. Further, as firearms researcher William B. Edwards notes in his book, *Civil War Guns*, not only is there no record of a Union general killed at extreme-range during the "Red River Campaign, Louisiana, April, 1864," but the alleged victim, "General George Lainhart," did not exist!

This story may have been inspired by an 1896 letter in *The Confederate Veteran*, written by former CSA Captain F.S. Harris, which claimed that a Rebel sharpshooter, assisted by the range estimate of an engineer officer, had killed a Union general at an astounding 2,250 yards. Harris claimed, "A few days later a Northern paper announced the General _____, I forget the name, and several of his staff were killed by Rebel sharpshooters at long range." Having done my best to confirm that incident and come up empty-handed, I, too, doubt that it ever happened.

When firing beyond 700 yards, Union sharpshooters employed heavy "telescope" rifles, which proved remarkably accurate. ("A Good Shot" by Dale Gallon, printed with permission, © Dale Gallon Historical Art.)

the Rebel sharpshooters dodged—then the second element shot, and their rounds arrived just as the "Johnnies" raised their heads, to deadly effect.

Ever-resourceful sharpshooters accepted the likelihood of their muzzle smoke being spotted and began displacing—that is, firing a shot and moving to another firing position—to protect themselves from counterfire. One clever Rebel sharpshooter, realizing that Yankee infantrymen had a psychological need to shoot back at something, propped up a body near his firing position to draw away their fire. The ruse would have worked except a Berdan Sharpshooter could see the truth through the magnified image of his scope and aimed at the live infantryman.

Even amid the fire of a general engagement, according to Union veterans, they could distinguish the whistling sound of a Whitworth bullet in flight—probably reflecting its distinct shape—and possibly even back-trace the hidden gunman's general direction.

Detecting a well-hidden sharpshooter could require a bit of investigative ingenuity. At Chancellorsville in 1863, when other means of spotting a Rebel sharpshooter failed, a Union sharpshooter employed a novel technique:

> "His bullet struck into the bank, and instantly our sharpshooter ran his ramrod down the hole made by the Johnnie's ball, then lay down on his back and sighted along the ramrod. He accordingly perceived from the direction that his game was on top of a thick bushy elm tree about 100 yards in the front. It was then the work of less than a second to aim his long telescopic rifle at that tree and crack she went. Down tumbled Mr. Johnnie like a great crow out of his nest, and we had no more trouble from that source."

When every other technique failed, there was still luring the sharpshooter's fire in hopes of spotting a puff of smoke or movement in a treetop. Most commonly, this involved displaying hats or items of clothing. A Confederate officer "had some sand bags removed from the wall, leaving two holes, at each of which a marksman with a Whitworth rifle stood ready to fire." Then a hat on a ramrod drew the unfortunate sniper's fire and, with it, his demise. In a more elaborate version, some Union sharpshooters "rigged up a stick with a hat and coat and shoved it out across a roadway, when instantly a report was heard and a bullet passed through the coat." This, too, drew an instant response from four sharpshooters, the Rebel "receiving his quietus."

On 24 May 1864, the *New York Herald* described an amazing counter-sharpshooter engagement, in which one unnamed Union marksman "would take a position behind a tree, select a spot where he knew a Rebel sharpshooter was concealed, and cover it with his gun" while his partner "would step out quickly in plain view of the Rebel, who would raise up and fire, only to fall back dead or wounded." By purposely exposing himself, the sharpshooter enabled his comrade to kill "no less than a half-dozen Rebel sharpshooters." This was no tall tale. Civil War records reveal that the Medal of Honor was presented to Corporal Follett Johnson of the 60th New York Infantry for having "exposed himself to the fire of a Confederate sharpshooter, thus drawing fire upon himself and enabling his comrade to shoot the sharpshooter."

The Medal of Honor also was awarded to Private Delano Morey of the 82nd Ohio Infantry for dealing with two Confederate sharpshooters. In Morey's case, he realized there would be a short pause while the gunmen reloaded, so he rushed the sharpshooters—"with an empty gun"—and captured both of them. "When they saw me coming on the full run," he later recalled, "they hastened to load their guns, but I was a little too quick for them." Similarly, Corporal Henderson Howard of the 11th Pennsylvania Reserves single-handedly rushed several sharpshooters, bayoneting them and prevailing despite sustaining three wounds.

Conventional infantry often dealt death blows to sharpshooters, sometimes delivered in a sophisticated way and sometimes not. After receiving a series of well-aimed shots from a distant wood line at Ellis' Ford, Virginia, a Union commander "ordered a volley fired, which must have taken the Reb by surprise, as he was found on their approach in a sprawling position at the foot of the tree, pretty much used up."

On other occasions, selective rifle fire did the trick. After "a crowd of Rebel sharpshooters annoyed us . . . by their constant firing at us through the night," a Captain Williams of Company D, 16th Illinois Cavalry, organized a detail of his regiment's finest riflemen. Stalking their way in the darkness to good overwatch positions, they could not see the sharpshooters, "but every time they would shoot, some of us would let them have one." By dawn, these select marksmen had eliminated the sharpshooters.

The 27th Massachusetts Regiment of Volunteer Infantry maintained a handful of counter-sharpshooters, ready to be called on whenever needed. "We soon acquainted ourselves with the positions and tricks of the enemy's sharpshooters, who, like many of our men, were in the trees, picking off any who showed their heads above the defenses." As many as a dozen riflemen replied to each sharpshooter's shot, focusing well-aimed fire to eliminate their foe.

Angered by continuing sharpshooter fire at Cold Harbor, CSA Brigadier General William Pender rode up to an artillery battery, recruited a dozen select rifle shots, and then went after the hidden Yankee. After "winding up" the one who had shot at General Pender, the Rebel marksmen helped themselves to his boots, clothing, and food, their own being in short supply.

SHARPSHOOTER VERSUS SHARPSHOOTER

Ultimately, the most effective means of countering a sharpshooter was pitting another sharp-shooter against him. "In such cases," wrote Captain Stevens of Berdan's Sharpshooters, "calls would be made for a detail of sharp shooters, who would be gone sometimes for several days before return-ing to camp, always, however, being successful in removing the trouble."

Confederate sharpshooters, too, were called in to duel their more troublesome Union counterparts. When the 1st Texas Volunteer Infantry, which had no long-range rifles, had "a lot of trouble" from Yankee sharpshooters, General John Hood asked General James Longstreet for assistance. He dispatched a sharpshooter named Serrell who "soon located the Yank and sneaked up near enough to make certain of his first shot." Not only did Serrell kill him, but he carried away the sharpshooter's rifle and all his gear.

When a Rebel sharpshooter killed a Berdan marksman during the Yorktown siege, Colonel Berdan personally spotted his firing position and then dispatched six sharpshooters to hunt the Rebel down, declaring, "They must put a stop to such work of the enemy." This became an overnight effort, with the Union men stalking forward in darkness and then awaiting dawn with their rifles trained on the sharpshooter's position. Soon after daylight the Confederate raised his head for the last time.

Union sharpshooters at Fort Wagner, South Carolina, maneuver against their Rebel counterparts.

"Thus was the colonel's order faithfully carried out," notes the Berdan unit history.

There were many similar incidents of hunters and hunted. So elated was the Confederate commander at Battery Wagner, South Carolina, to have a Union sharpshooter killed that it was his first item in a lengthy dispatch, which began, "I have the honor to report that our sharpshooters on yesterday afternoon killed one of the enemy's sharpshooters and wounded another."

Many accomplished sharpshooters who had withstood the test of battle and the full panoply of enemy countermeasures—artillery fire, cavalry assaults, infantry volleys—found it impossible to resist the deliberate, calculated efforts of an enemy sharpshooter who understood his foe. Francis M. Ferguson, a sharpshooter with the 4th Regiment of Kentucky Infantry, "was a brave man, and . . . one of the best shots in the division." During the Atlanta Campaign alone, he'd reportedly shot 25 Union officers, "principally mounted." With that kind of record, Ferguson likely drew the attention of his Union counterparts, for shortly afterward he was shot dead by one well-aimed bullet to his brain.

Also during the Atlanta Campaign, at Kennesaw Mountain, sharpshooter Henry Goldsmith of the 16th South Carolina was shot dead, "while taking aim at a sharpshooter on the other side." He, too, was much accomplished and "a fine shot, the second best in the regiment."

Whether employed as here—to hunt enemy sharpshooters—or to suppress artillery, eliminate leaders, or skirmish the flanks, sharpshooters contributed to every major action of the Civil War, sometimes tipping the scales to victory or defeat at the most critical moment. To better recognize how these marksmen made their contributions, we need to look beyond tactics and techniques and view sharpshooting in the wider context of the war's most significant battles. At these critical times, I have discovered, the contribution of precision sharpshooter fire was much greater than previously realized.

PART
3 SHARPSHOOTERS IN BATTLE

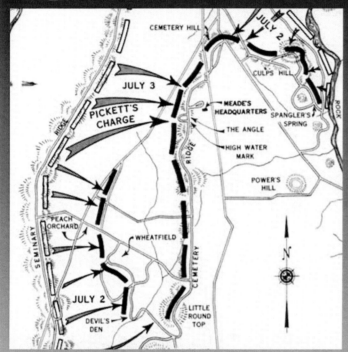

CHAPTER SIX

Bloody Days: Antietam and Fredericksburg

The great majority of Civil War casualties, without question, were inflicted by artillery and ordinary rifle fire. Though no such reliable statistics exist, it's fairly certain that less than 5 percent of combat losses—perhaps only 2 or 3 percent—resulted from the deliberate fire of sharpshooters.

Both by mission and training, however, the goal of these few precision shooters was not to inflict mass casualties. Rather, it was to selectively engage important targets at critical times and places, and in that, as we'll soon see, they succeeded well beyond what has generally been realized.

Let us consider, then, the dramatic and sometimes decisive effects this tiny band of elite marksmen and their well-aimed shots achieved in four battles—Antietam and Fredericksburg in this chapter, and Gettysburg and Vicksburg later—to better understand their impact on the war as a whole.

ANTIETAM

In his first invasion of the North, in early September 1862, General Robert E. Lee bypassed the Union's Washington-area troop concentrations to boldly ford the

BATTLE FIELD OF SHARPSBURG OR ANTIETAM

☐ FEDERAL WORKS
▬ CONFEDERATE.WORKS

Potomac River 60 miles to the northeast. With Lee's 55,000-man army threatening Baltimore and Philadelphia, Union General George B. McClellan hastily assembled an army of 84,000 men and marched north to head him off. Realizing that Lee must transit the Blue Ridge Mountains through two key passes, Turner's Gap and Fox's Gap, McClellan hurried Major General Ambrose Burnside forward with two Union Army corps, resulting in the first clash on 14 September.

Finding the Confederates already there, Burnside's IX Corps commander, Major General Jesse Reno, assaulted the hill mass at Fox's Gap. Delays slowed his advance, and then the determined Rebel defenders bogged it further. At 6 P.M. Reno rode the lines, encouraging his troops, and then paused with several officers to observe enemy positions. Lifting a telescope to his eye, General Reno had no sooner spotted them than a sharpshooter's slug struck him. "He fell," a *Harper's Weekly* reporter wrote, "and, from the first, appeared to have a knowledge that he could not survive the wound. . . ."

One historian observed this was a critical moment, as "confusion spread among Union regiments, some of which were fresh in battle and were at that time being moved to the front." The 21st New York, fighting its way up a ravine, mistakenly turned in the wrong direction; fortunately, the 2nd U.S. Sharpshooter Regiment went forward in its place, dealing considerable destruction with its rapid-loading Sharps rifles. By dark, despite Reno's death, the Rebels had been pushed off the hill. Confederate General D.H. Hill announced that Reno was "killed by a happy shot from the 23rd North Carolina," with the sharpshooter later identified as Sergeant Charles Bennett, who'd fired "at long range."

In the opening phase of Antietam, a Confederate sharpshooter killed Union General Jesse Reno, the IX Corps commander.

Losing control of the mountain passes, General Lee fell back 5 miles, taking up defensive positions just beyond Antietam Creek, near Sharpsburg. The methodical, ever-cautious McClellan followed, taking two full days to bring his Army of the Potomac into position. When McClellan attacked, early on 17 September, it began as a multiple corps assault from Lee's north, which unhinged as quickly as it began. At 7:35 A.M., Major General Joseph K.F. Mansfield, commander of the XII Corps, was mortally wounded by a Confederate sharpshooter's bullet.

This was bad enough, but soon afterward his adjacent Union Corps commander, Major General Joseph Hooker, also was seriously wounded by a Confederate sharpshooter. The targeting of Major General Hooker was made simpler because he rode a "conspicuous white horse."

Union Major General Joseph K.F. Mansfield was killed by a Rebel sharpshooter just as the main battle began at Antietam.

Imagine the chaos: in only four days, the Army of the Potomac had lost half its corps commanders, all to sharpshooters. The effect at Antietam was serious and immediate. "The loss of two fighting corps commanders," a West Point textbook explains, "left no one in overall control of McClellan's 'main attack' on the Confederate left." Coordination fell apart; command and control fell apart. Units advanced piecemeal, allowing General Lee to counter them one at a time. One isolated unit was the 2nd U.S. Sharpshooter Regiment, which lost 66 men but poured such heavy, accurate fire into a sunken road—"Bloody Lane"— that the men inflicted several times their own losses. The Sharpshooter's commander, Colonel Henry A.V. Post, was severely wounded and would not return to active service.

Riding a "conspicuous white horse," Union Major General Joseph Hooker was seriously wounded early in the Battle of Antietam.

Looking west across Antietam Bridge. Rebel sharpshooters in the facing building (200 yards) and ridgeline (500 yards) shot hundreds of assaulting soldiers.

A Great Sharpshooter Ambush

The accuracy of Whitworth rifles was soon known and feared. But no engagement so well demonstrated the rifle's decisive effect when employed wisely as a November 1863 ambush on the Tennessee River.

At the time, the Union Army was occupying Chattanooga, Tennessee, and relied on a supply road that paralleled the Tennessee River. Some 12 miles west of Chattanooga, across the river from Raccoon Mountain, Union wagon trains were virtually pinned against the river and vulnerable to fire from the southern bank, some 250 yards away.

Confederate General James Longstreet dispatched a select handful of sharpshooters armed with scoped Whitworth rifles to hide among the rocks and trees of the river's south bank and lie in wait. The situation being unhurried—and with no guards on the Yankee side of the river—the sharpshooters had plenty of time to set their scopes for the exact range. They may even have fired a few spotting rounds.

The resulting ambush, witnessed by Frank Vizetelly, a correspondent-artist of the *Illustrated London News*, can only be termed "catastrophic."

Cheering in exultation, Rebel sharpshooters celebrate the long-range ambush of a Union wagon train on the Tennessee River.

The first well-aimed shots knocked down the lead wagon's mules, blocking the narrow road. There simply wasn't room for the other wagons to turn around, nor could they back up. The Union security escort, "after firing a few shots in return, fled panic-stricken." Methodically—"in a leisurely manner" one sharpshooter later wrote—the Whitworth riflemen tore apart the trapped convoy, "leaving the road choked with dead and dying men and mules and overturned wagons."

In triumph, Vizetelly reported, the handful of sharpshooters stood up and their "exulted shouts" echoed off Raccoon Mountain, an image he later drew for his newspaper. The Longstreet sharpshooters' victory compelled Union logisticians to shift future wagon trains to more protected but less convenient routes.

With fighting in the north tapering off, action shifted to the south where Major General Ambrose Burnside's four divisions were massing to assault a bridge on Antietam Creek. Had Burnside's forces struck simultaneously with Hooker and Mansfield in the north, the field should have been theirs. But Burnside was not ordered to launch his assault until 10 A.M., allowing plenty of time for Confederate sharpshooters to occupy buildings less than 200 yards beyond the creek and position themselves on a wide hillcrest some 500 yards west. Even worse, the Union approach to the bridge, a dirt road, paralleled the creek across open ground, allowing flanking fire as the men rushed it.

The first assault, led by the 11th Connecticut Regiment, took heavy, accurate rifle fire; some 139 men fell, including Colonel Henry Kingsbury, the regimental commander.

An hour later came a second assault by fresh troops, and the result was the same: Union soldiers clogging the bridge and drawing an intense concentration of sharpshooter fire. Finally, the third assault, launched at 12:30, made it across, forcing back the Rebel sharpshooters, whose well-aimed

The Day They Shot Lincoln—Almost

In July 1864, as Union armies neared the Confederate capitol at Richmond, CSA General Jubal Early was ordered to launch a diversionary attack toward Washington in hopes he could draw away Northern forces. Striking from Virginia's Shenandoah Valley, Early's feint became a successful offensive that caught Lincoln's generals off guard and made it to the capitol's defenses, within sight of the uncompleted capitol dome.

The spectacle of combat within earshot of the White House drew out Lincoln and his entourage to Fort Stevens, one of 68 forts ringing the District of Columbia, located at the intersection of today's Quakenbos and 13th Streets. The president, famous for shooting rifles on the White House lawn and riding horseback among his generals, did not hesitate to climb atop a parapet to watch skirmishing in the distance, silhouetting himself perfectly against the skyline. Of course, so perfect a target drew sharpshooter fire, with rounds zinging the air. An eyewitness wrote in his diary:

> "The enemy was firing lively from the bushes in front of the fort and it was dangerous for any person to look over the parapet, but the President was bound he would look over and see what was going on. Soon a sharpshooter fired at him, and he dodged, in doing so tipped over the pass box on which he was sitting and tumbled down."

President Abraham Lincoln at the parapet of Fort Stevens, perfectly silhouetted for a sharpshooter's fire.

Wartime photo of Fort Stevens, located on the edge of Washington, D.C.

That near miss deflected off a cannon barrel and seriously wounded Charles V. Crawford, surgeon of the 102nd Pennsylvania Volunteer Infantry. Prior to the president's arrival, two men had been killed at Fort Stevens by sharpshooter fire. Mary Todd Lincoln, the president's wife, two years earlier had lost a brother, Captain Alexander A. Todd, to a sharpshooter, so the president should have had a respect for the danger of precision rifle shots.

As it was, Lincoln only abandoned the parapet when a young aide shouted, "Get down, you damn fool!" At the time, the youthful officer was no one of prominence, but many years afterward he became respected as one of the country's finest Supreme Court Justices, Oliver Wendell Holmes.

On the Confederate side, there was no inkling of who these men in civilian clothing were that appeared in the sharpshooters' sights. Firing from where today's Walter Reed Medical Center stands, Confederate Captain Robert E. Park noted, "the sharpshooters . . . suppose they were 'Home Guards' composed of Treasury, Post Office and other Department Clerks."

Soon afterward, with the federal army rapidly reinforcing—and his diversion having succeeded—General Early withdrew. "We didn't take Washington," Early told his staff, "but we scared Abe Lincoln like hell."

shots had delayed Burnside for three critical hours. Another delay followed while ammunition was brought forward; then, just as Burnside was about to renew his attack, a fresh Confederate division arrived and forced him to fall back to Antietam Creek.

While this was happening, four Confederate generals conferred on a facing ridge, inspiring a Yankee sharpshooter to attempt a long-range shot. It connected with Brigadier General Lawrence O'Bryan Branch, a brigade commander in Hill's Division, killing this son of a distinguished family that included governors of both Florida and North Carolina. Reminiscent of the shooting of Union General Reno three days earlier, Branch was shot "as he was in the act of raising field glasses to his eyes."

CSA Brigadier General Lawrence O'Bryan Branch was killed by a Union sharpshooter too late to make any difference at Antietam.

Branch's death did not alter the battle's outcome, for the die already had been cast. The Battle of Antietam had cost 25,000 Union and Confederate soldiers killed and wounded, with no decisive result. Many historians blame McClellan's ineptness for failing to achieve victory despite a substantial advantage of numbers. However, in addition to Lee's superior operational art, his army's wiser use of sharpshooters must be considered. Decapitating the Union Army's northern flank leadership in the opening minutes of battle, combined with delaying Burnside's advance a full three hours, had an effect far disproportionate to the number of marksmen involved.

The Union Army, by contrast, misemployed its sharpshooters throughout the fight. The 2nd U.S. Sharpshooter Regiment was fielded as ordinary infantry, while the 1st Regiment was held in reserve throughout the battle. Imagine the effect if they had been called on to counter the enemy sharpshooters delaying Burnside's forces at Antietam bridge. Incredibly, the 1st Company of Andrews Sharpshooters, armed with heavy telescope rifles, was pushed forward as assault troops—and they died by droves, cut down by rapid-reloading Rebel infantrymen. Their commander, Captain John Saunders, and executive officer, Lieutenant William Berry, were among the 11 dead, along with another 21 wounded—more than half their strength. Even with these losses, the Massachusetts marksmen managed to put a Confederate artillery battery out of action for most of the day. The same thing happened to the 2nd Minnesota Sharpshooters, whose 29 men fought as ordinary infantry, losing 20 "within a space of time not exceeding 10 minutes."

FREDERICKSBURG

The Union counterstroke following Antietam, launched some 10 weeks later, involved a south-ward thrust from Washington aimed at the Confederate capital at Richmond. The Army of the Potomac, now commanded by General Burnside, massed 50 miles south of Washington, on the north side of the Rappahannock River, opposite the town of Fredericksburg. Burnside planned to cross his

120,000 men on float bridges on 26 November, well before Lee's 85,000-man Army of Northern Virginia could arrive to oppose him.

Delay begot delay, however, and by the morning of 10 December, when Union engineers finally began assembling their three pontoon bridges, the situation had changed dramatically. The 250-yard-wide Rappahannock River was covered by massed Confederate sharpshooters from Brigadier General William Barksdale's Mississippi Brigade, who'd heavily fortified every cellar and stone building along Fredericksburg's mile-wide river-front. And beyond, stretched along the hills a mile deeper, stood Lee's entire army.

At sunrise on 11 December, men of the 50th New York Engineers began assembling and shoving into position sections of pontoon bridges, and, as quickly as the fog lifted,

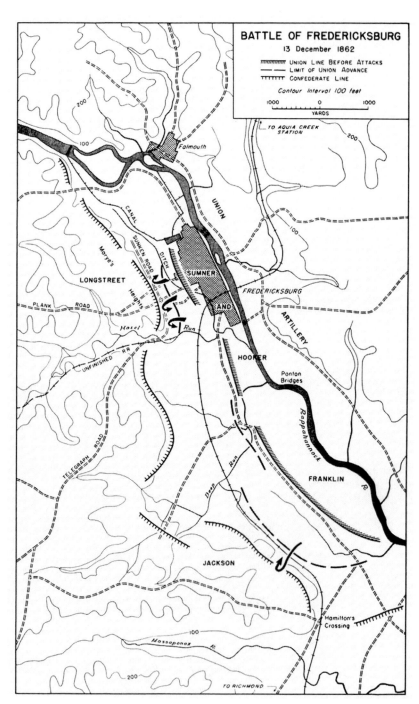

Above: Under heavy fire from Barksdale's Mississippi Brigade, Union troops cross the Rappahannock River at Fredericksburg.

Right: Delayed a half day by Barksdale's well-entrenched sharpshooters, Union troops finally storm ashore at Fredericksburg.

The 19th and 20th Massachusetts Regiments suffered heavy casualties in the streets of Fredericksburg.

Few last words can compete with those of Union Major General John Sedgwick, who, seeking to reassure artillery-men that long-distance enemy sharpshooter fire was more an irritant than a danger, stood openly beside them and uttered his famous quote.

The setting was Spotsylvania, Virginia, the date 9 May 1864. One of the Union Army's most senior officers, Sedgwick commanded the VI Corps, incorporating three infantry divisions and an artillery brigade, approximately one-quarter of the entire Army of the Potomac. Dissatisfied with the way his artillery was arrayed, Sedgwick wanted to reposition a battery, located at an angle in the lines.

"Seriously, general, I beg of you, not to go to that angle," his chief of staff, Brigadier General Martin McMahon, requested. "Every officer who has shown himself there has been hit, both today and yesterday." Sedgwick, who had been in action since the opening days of the war, perhaps had grown inured to danger or, as McMahon thought, too quickly forgot the warning.

When Sedgwick later approached the guns, a sharp-shooter's bullet whizzed past, sending a crew scrambling for cover. Sedgwick laughed and asked, "What? Men dodging this way for single bullets! What will you do when they open fire along the whole line? I am ashamed of you. They could-n't hit an elephant at this distance." Seconds later, a sol-dier walked by the general and another bullet flashed past, sending the young soldier diving to the ground. Sedgwick touched him with the toe of his boot and said, "Why, my man, I am ashamed of you, dodging that

Major General John Sedgwick, commanding the Union VI corps, killed by Rebel sharpshooter Ben Powell at Spotsylvania.

way," and then repeated his words: "They couldn't hit an elephant at this dis-tance."

The young soldier stood, saluted, and explained that he'd previously sur-vived fire by dodging. "I believe in dodging," he said. Sedgwick laughed and replied, "All right, my man; go to your place."

Again, a single bullet zipped in, this time "closing with a dull, heavy stroke," and Sedgwick, "the most beloved general in the Army of the Potomac," fell over, killed instantly by a long-range Whitworth's bullet that struck just below his left eye.

On the Confederate side, Rebel sharpshooter Berry Benson heard shouting far down the line, which raced his way like a locomotive, growing in pitch and volume until he heard, "Grant's wounded! Grant's wounded! Grant's wounded!" Then "Grant's dead! Grant's dead!" Of course, it was not General Grant, although a senior Union officer had died.

Georgia sharpshooter Benson believed that the fatal shot was fired by Ben Powell, using a Whitworth rifle. The day after Sedgwick was shot, Benson

Only one day after General Sedgwick's death, Union Brigadier General Thomas Stevenson, com-manding the 1st Division, also fell to a sharpshooter at Spotsylvania.

sought out Powell and actually had a chance to fire that very rifle, commenting only that "it kicked powerfully." Confederate Major William Dunlop, in his authoritative *Lee's Sharpshooters*, also attributes the shot to Ben Powell. As Dunlop wrote, "Powell reported at once that he had killed a Federal general, but we knew not his name until it came out a few days later in the Northern papers. . . ."

The affable but entirely competent Sedgwick was sorely missed. Learning of his death, General Ulysses S. Grant remarked that "to lose Sedgwick was as bad as to lose a whole division of infantry."

A statue of Sedgwick was dedicated at West Point in 1868, and to this day academically challenged cadets—at midnight, before finals—sneak to the statue and spin "Uncle John's" spur rowels, in belief his spirit will help them pass.

Barksdale's sharpshooters began dropping them, one after another after another. These chosen riflemen—drawn from the 13th, 17th, 18th, and 21st Mississippi Infantry Regiments—made life such hell that the engineers had to abandon the half-built bridges.

Thirty-six Union artillery pieces poured shells into the waterfront buildings, but they had little effect. As quickly as the engineers returned, the Rebel sharpshooters again dropped them in droves. Adding more artillery fire did not work. Hours dragged past.

Finally, at 2:30 that afternoon, the 7th Michigan Regiment boarded boats and, supported by a heavy artillery barrage, paddled across the Rappahannock. Masked by smoke, enough Michigan men made it ashore to secure a toehold. The 19th and 20th Massachusetts Regiments followed, forcing back the sharpshooters and allowing the bridging to continue. According to Private Henry Ropes of the 20th, "The orders to the whole brigade was to bayonet every armed man we found firing from a house, this being, I believe, contrary to the rules of war, but it was of course not obeyed."

Engaging the withdrawing Rebel sharpshooters, the Union troops advanced into a carefully planned urban defense, causing "the most useless slaughter I ever witnessed," wrote Corporal A.W. Greeley of the 19th Massachusetts. Within 10 minutes, advancing one city block, the 20th Regiment lost 97 men.

Wyman White of Berdan's Sharpshooters observed:

> "General Burnside was a loyal, patriotic man but he ought to have known . . . just what would be the outcome of crossing the river right into the face of an impregnable position defended by as brave an army as ever in battle, commanded by generals of high standing."

The battle raged for two more days. Far more Union soldiers died after crossing the Rappahannock, but the delay achieved by Barksdale's sharpshooters had so upset the Federal timetable that nothing quite synchronized afterward. By the afternoon of 13 December, an estimated 10,000 Union soldiers had been killed or wounded, double the number of Confederate casualties.

Killing the Men Who Killed Polk

It was not every day that a three-star general was killed in action. Confederate Lieutenant General Leonidas Polk—nicknamed "Bishop Polk" because he'd once been an Episcopal bishop—was observing Union positions alongside Generals Joseph Johnston and William Hardee near Marietta, Georgia, when an incoming Union shell detonated beside him. Hardee and Johnston escaped injury, but Polk was killed, one of only three Confederate corps commanders to die in the war.

There was no gloating on the Union side; however, the commander of the 5th Indiana Battery that fired the fatal shot, Captain Peter Simonson, was justifiably congratulated for a fine job.

Whether Simonson was purposely targeted by sharpshooters to avenge the death of Polk is not known. But what is known is what happened a mere 48 hours later.

The same dispatch in which Brigadier General W. Grose, commanding the Union's 3rd Brigade of the 1st Division, reported General Polk's death—just two sentences later—also stated, "On this day [16 June], we had the sad misfortune to lose the brave and gallant officer, Captain Simonson, our chief of artillery."

"Bishop Polk," CSA Lieutenant General Leonidas Polk, was killed near Marietta, Georgia, by a shot from the 5th Indiana Battery.

"While laying out a position for a battery," another report elaborates, "Capt. Peter Simonson, Fifth Indiana Battery, was instantly killed by a sharpshooter. This was an irreparable loss to the division."

Confederate Lieutenant L.D. Young of the Orphan Brigade, an eyewitness to Polk's death, later wrote that the shot that killed Captain Simonson was fired by a Kerr-armed marksman from Lieutenant George Hector Burton's Sharpshooters. Whether that was a chance encounter or a deliberate attack, however, Young did not say.

CHAPTER SEVEN

Three Days at Gettysburg

Commanding the Army of the Potomac's I, III, and XI Corps, Major General John Reynolds was the highest-ranking Union officer killed at Gettysburg.

Geneneral Robert E. Lee's second invasion of the North brought the 75,000-man Army of Northern Virginia into Pennsylvania's sleepy Cumberland Valley. The Army of the Potomac's newest commander, General George Meade, hurried his 85,000 Union troops northward, unsure of Lee's location. The two armies stumbled into each other just west of Gettysburg on 1 July 1863.

Rapidly, both sides began massing. General John F. Reynolds, the highly respected commander of the Army of the Potomac's I, III, and XI Corps, rode forward to personally position his arriving units. The fight had hardly begun when a Confederate sharpshooter noticed a distinguished rider escorted by officers and giving commands—that's all the Rebel marksman needed. His well-aimed shot instantly killed the highest-ranking Union officer to fall at Gettysburg. Adding to the confusion of an unclear, developing situation, Reynolds' untimely death and resulting command disruption contributed to the Confederates prevailing in that first day's fight.

By dawn of 2 July, the Union Army had fallen back and

was concentrating forces along defensive terrain on the 2-mile-long, north-south Cemetery Ridge, and in the northeast, atop Culp's Hill. The nearest Confederate troops were the 5th Alabama's sharpshooters, who fired upon the Federals from buildings they'd occupied in the town of Gettysburg, 425 yards north of the Yankee's northernmost position. In the attic at 309 Baltimore Street, a dozen marksmen had knocked out bricks as firing portals, while more sharpshooters reinforced a garret window at 401 Baltimore Street, and still more took up positions at 404 Baltimore Street, as well as behind and between several adjacent buildings.

Meanwhile, Lee's army fanned out along Seminary Ridge, parallel to and approximately a mile west of the Army of the Potomac. Significantly, this meant that the bulk of the sharpshooters of both armies were well beyond their rifles' maximum range, facing each other across open ground too devoid of cover even for rifle pits.

By the morning of 2 July, the 1st and 2nd U.S. Sharpshooter Regiments were arrayed at the southern end of the Union lines, skirmishing to the west. It was a stroke of luck, for they chanced upon CSA General James Longstreet's 30,000-strong assault force, hidden in the woods. Though Colonel Berdan had only 300 sharpshooters, he attacked and so startled the Rebel force that it delayed Longstreet's attack by 40 minutes—barely enough time for General Meade to reinforce his vulnerable southern flank.

Fighting erupted in the Federal center and south, with tens of thousands of rifles firing, making it all but impossible to distinguish between a single well-aimed shot dropping its target and simply a stray bullet striking an unfortunate soul. Confederate General William Barksdale was said to have been killed by a Union sharpshooter, shot off "his fine white charger," but that's hard to determine. Colonel Edward Cross, commanding a Union brigade, was almost certainly killed by a Confederate sharpshooter. Fighting raged with so many flying bullets that it all merged into one unending explosion.

Pressed heavily in the south, Union forces had to

CSA General William Barksdale, shot off "his fine white charger," was believed killed by a Union sharpshooter.

The Oldest Gettysburg Sharpshooter

Soon after the initial clashes at Gettysburg, the town's elderly constable, John Burns, presented himself to Major Thomas Chamberlain of the just arriving 150th Pennsylvania Regiment. Borrowing a rifle from a wounded soldier, the 69-year-old veteran of the War of 1812 volunteered to sharpshoot for his fellow Pennsylvanians. Eying the elderly man, Major Chamberlain thanked him for his patriotism and suggested he try another unit, such as the nearby Iron Brigade.

Had Chamberlain inquired a bit more he might not have been so hasty. For Burns had not merely carried a rifle four decades earlier but had fought with distinction at Plattsburg, Queenstown, and Lundy's Lane, at the latter helping seize a battery of enemy guns. As the local townspeople knew, the old rifleman was a crack shot.

Despite the rejection, Burns approached the Iron Brigade and found a more receptive officer in Colonel Langhorne Wister, who warned, "But you have no ammunition."

"Yes I have," the clear-eyed veteran announced, slapping his pockets.

"Do you know how to shoot?" Wister asked, the sound of heavy firing growing by the minute.

"Give me a chance," swore Burns, "and I will show you whether I can shoot or not."

Sent forward to the 7th Wisconsin Volunteer Infantry Regiment, Burns demonstrated his skill, firing with precision and deliberation. His uncanny accuracy attracted the regiment's executive officer, Lieutenant Colonel John Callis, who "sent him a silver-mounted rifle that had been captured from the enemy in the Battle of Antietam." Espying a distinguished Rebel officer "riding a beautiful gray horse," the elderly Burns took careful aim and "that beautiful charger was soon seen galloping riderless over the field, and the old hero was saluted by three cheers from the soldiers who were watching him."

Much of that day Burns spent firing that heavy Confederate rifle, and, it was believed, his nearly every shot brought down an enemy soldier. Then, growing reckless and exposing himself, he was struck by two musket balls, and as he lay wounded, a third slammed into him. Regaining his feet, Burns fired yet again and was struck by a fourth bullet, fired by Rebel soldiers overrunning his position. Unconscious, he was passed for dead, and afterward the Confederates almost executed him for having fought in civilian clothes—but the great battle swirling about him was over before that could be accomplished.

While Burns slowly healed, word of his courageous sharpshooting spread, capturing the public's imagination. Soon, newspapers called him the "Hero of Gettysburg" and no veteran of that decisive action garnered more respect. When President Abraham Lincoln arrived to deliver his famous Gettysburg Address, he sent for Burns, but the humble old man thought people were pulling his leg and refused to go. Overcoming his protests, neighbors led him to the president, who spoke with the old sharpshooter at length and then "walked with him arm in arm through the streets." Until John Burns' death in 1872, visitors to the great battlefield often called on him, delighted to meet the oldest sharpshooter to fight at Gettysburg.

John Burns, at 69 years, was the eldest sharpshooter at Gettysburg.

give ground, falling back toward a prominent hill, Little Round Top, unoccupied but for a 24-man signal detachment. Union Major General Gouverneur Warren, chief engineer of the Army of the Potomac, arrived at the scene, instantly grasped Little Round Top's strategic value—its heights commanded the battlefield's southern end—and diverted passing Union units to its defense. Had Berdan's men not delayed Longstreet's attack, and had not General Warren aggressively occupied Little Round Top, the battle may well have been lost.

As it was, Longstreet's soldiers fought their way to within 100 yards of the hill's pinnacle before they were thrown back by arriving Union infantry and artillery. And at that moment Confederate

Dead Rebel sharpshooters in the Devil's Den, afterward called the "Slaughter Pen."

A Rebel sharpshooter's view of Little Round Top from the Devil's Den—exactly 522 yards to the crest.

Brigadier General Stephen Weed, commander, 3rd Brigade, 2nd Division, was shot dead on Little Round Top by a Rebel sharpshooter.

Lieutenant Charles Hazlett was kneeling over the mortally wounded Brigadier General Stephen Weed, trying to hear his last words, when he too was killed by a sharpshooter.

sharpshooters arrived below the hill, taking cover in a jumble of truck-sized boulders, in so eerie a setting that it was known as the Devil's Den.

On the heights of Little Round Top—exactly 522 yards away, a certainty because I personally measured it with a laser rangefinder—General Warren stood, holding binoculars, silhouetted against the afternoon sky. A Rebel sharpshooter aimed at the distinct figure, squeezed, and saw him fall. Wounded, but not seriously, Warren would survive.

From the cool shadows of the Devil's Den, another Rebel sharpshooter made

Who Shot General Reynolds?

That Union Major General John F. Reynolds died in the opening clash of the Battle of Gettysburg is beyond question. That he was the victim of a sharpshooter's bullet is almost universally accepted. That Reynolds was shot by Ben Thorpe or John Hendrix or Frank Wood or . . .? Well, a number of Confederates claimed the shot, though none offered verification or an eyewitness to support his claim.

Revisionist historians and Civil War buffs attempting to demonstrate their superior knowledge have pecked away at the sharpshooter claim for many years, despite almost all reports at the time attributing the shot to a Rebel sharpshooter. While nearly all these critics lack any familiarity with firearms, and especially with long-range shooting, they're expert enough to insist that this piece of woods or that barn was too distant, the angle of the shot was too sharp, or there were too many trees and so on, and then offer their own pet theories. After dismissing the known claimants—yet offering no evidence for his conclusion—one Gettysburg buff decided Reynolds was not even the victim of a sharpshooter since "it is much more fitting that a common infantryman may have brought the general's life to a close." What on earth does "more fitting" mean?

This period sketch depicts General Reynolds' death at Gettysburg, the victim, most authorities agree, of a Confederate sharpshooter.

Temporarily halting his mounted staff officers while waving arriving units to their locations, and with plenty of potential sharpshooter positions less than 500 yards away, Reynolds—resplendent in the uniform of a general officer—quite naturally drew the attention of a hostile marksman. His killing wound, a single shot to the neck, fits the modus operandi of a sharpshooter attempting a head shot or employing a bit too much elevation for a center-mass shot. Beware the revisionists who want to tinker with history.

out a prominent figure atop Little Round Top. He fired—mortally wounding the just-arrived Brigadier General Stephen Weed, commander of the 2nd Division's 3rd Brigade. As Weed fell, the commander of a Union artillery battery ran to his side, and, while attempting to hear his commander's final words, Lieutenant Charles Hazlett, too, was shot dead by a sharpshooter and fell atop General Weed. The range now well known, sharpshooter fire began impacting all across the hilltop while reinforcing Union soldiers frantically stacked rocks and logs for cover. Since they were looking downhill into the late afternoon's descending sun, the glare made aiming difficult for Union riflemen and sharpshooters.

A hundred yards south of where Weed and Hazlett had fallen, Brigadier General Strong Vincent, commanding the 3rd Brigade of the 1st Division, waved his men right and left on Little Round Top's slope—and collapsed from a fatal sharpshooter's bullet. Within sight of where General Vincent fell,

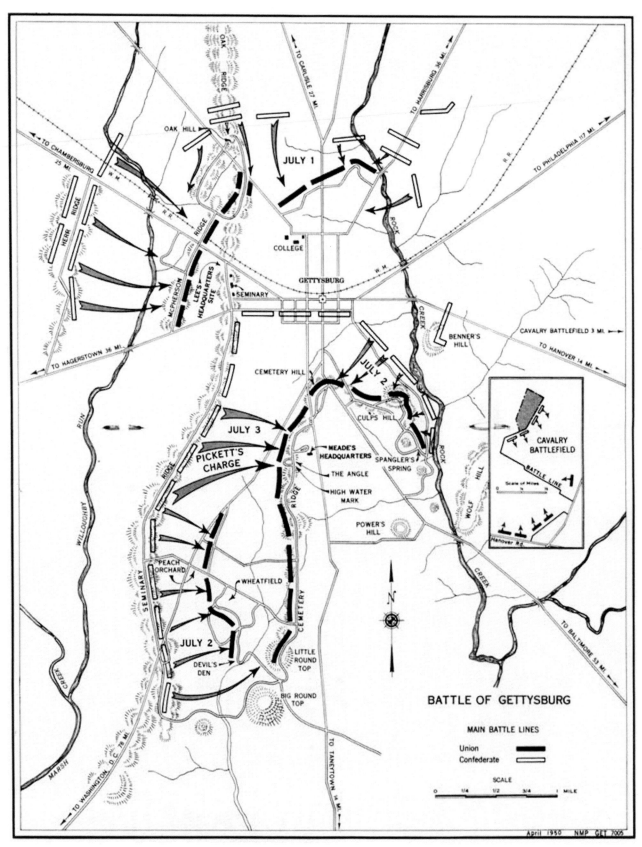

Critical fighting swarmed around Little Round Top and the Devil's Den (lower left). Pickett's Charge aimed for the Union center. General Reynolds was shot to the northwest.

Colonel Patrick O'Rourke, commander, 140th New York Infantry, was killed on Little Round Top by a Confederate sharpshooter.

Marking the spot where General Strong Vincent was mortally wounded, this tablet stands on Little Round Top's southeast slope.

Colonel Patrick O'Rourke, commanding the 140th New York Infantry, also was positioning his newly arrived men on Little Round Top when still another sharpshooter's bullet struck him dead. Five Union regiments, supported by at least three companies of Berdan's Sharpshooters, frantically fought off every attempt to seize Little Round Top and did their best to counter the Confederate sharpshooter fire.

From the immense granite boulders of the Devil's Den, Confederate sharpshooters continued to take their toll. Then a salvo of Union artillery slammed into the rocks, killing many marksmen with fragments and flying rocks and sheer concussion. It was not until 20 Berdan Sharpshooters finally rushed the Devil's Den and compelled the Rebels to surrender that at last, Little Round Top—and with it, the Union's southern flank—was secure. Expecting no quarter, the prisoners "begged lustily for their lives . . . until they learned that their captors were Berdan Sharpshooters," and they would not be killed.

The next morning, 3 July, found a fairly quiet battlefield. It was not until 1 P.M. that Confederate artillery let loose an hour-long barrage concentrated on the Union center, answered by an even heavier Union barrage. Then, at 2 P.M., some 12,000 Confederate infantrymen emerged from the woods of Seminary Ridge and arrayed for the largest frontal assault in American history. Upon signal, they advanced quick-time toward the Union lines, a bloody mile distant across open, relatively flat ground.

In Gettysburg's houses on Baltimore Street, Rebel sharpshooter commander Major Eugene Blackford had his instructions: "My orders were to fire incessantly without regard to ammunition." Before him, Blackford saw "100,000 [Union] men, all massed densely so that every shot from our side told." He directed his men to engage an artillery battery just 400 yards away, and the Union crews were

Close Calls

With hundreds of sharpshooters prowling battle-fields, senior officers inevitably came within their range, especially while reconnoitering or rousing their frontline troops to victory. In many instances, as we've examined, the result was fallen leaders, sometimes at critical times and places.

As well, there were numerous narrow escapes, inspiring speculative "might have beens." On 22 August 1862, General Robert E. Lee, commander of the Confederacy's Army of Northern Virginia, rode forward to personally survey the terrain at Second Manassas—and returned with a bloodied cheek, the mark of a hair's-breadth miss by a Union sharpshooter. The following spring, while riding along the Plank Road between Fredericksburg and Chancellorsville, Lee again appeared in a sharpshooter's sight, compelling him and General Thomas "Stonewall" Jackson to retire to better cover. Almost exactly a year

"LEE TO THE REAR!" Fearing Lee's exposure to enemy fire, Confederate soldiers halt their beloved leader. At least three times Lee appeared in Union sharpshooters' sights.

later, on 5 May 1864, "eight or ten [Union sharpshooters]" strayed behind Confederate lines and halted within view of General Lee. "Those adventurous blue coats, finding themselves in front of two brigades of Wilcox's division, made a rapid retreat," the Southern account concludes, "ignorant, most likely, that a very precious life lay for a moment at the mercy of their rifles."

General Ulysses S. Grant also narrowly survived enemy sharpshooter fire.

Lee's counterpart, General Ulysses S. Grant, was not immune from hazard. At Hatcher's Run, on 27 October 1864, General Grant, accompanied by General George Meade and his staff, rode forward to issue orders on a threatened flank. "General Grant, as was his constant practice," one history recalls, "wished to see the exact position of the enemy with his own eyes." No sooner had Grant halted than artillery fire accompanied by zinging sharpshooter's bullets impacted all around him—but he rode away, unhurt. An account in a Confederate newspaper, the *Charleston Mercury*, claims that Rebel sharpshooters narrowly missed Grant at Missionary Ridge on 17 September 1863, but that had to have been General George "Rock of Chickamauga" Thomas, for Grant was a thousand miles away.

Union General Daniel Sickles similarly had brushes with death by sharpshooter. At Chancellorsville, General Sickles and General David Birney met on a hill to view the fighting "in plain sight of the Rebels, when one of their sharpshooters marked them and fired with a target rifle," the *New York Herald* reported. The shot flashed harmlessly between the two generals, who repositioned to safer ground. At Ressacca, Georgia, on 12 May 1864, while "lounging under the trees" near an artillery battery, again Sickles drew long-range sharpshooter fire that came "unpleasantly close to Generals Sickles and [Major General Joseph] Hooker." Recall, too, that Hooker already had been wounded by a sharpshooter at Antietam, on 17 September 1862.

CSA General Nathan Bedford Forrest, the South's legendary

126   SHARPSHOOTING IN THE CIVIL WAR

Confederate Lieutenant General Richard Ewell joked when he was shot by a Union sharpshooter—in his wooden leg.

cavalry commander, almost met his doom via a Union sharpshooter, losing his mount at Fort Donelson to a bullet intended for his person. "The general was badly shaken," a Forrest biography notes, and perhaps explains why he later took up a rifle and personally shot a Yankee sharpshooter.

Perhaps the closest "miss" by a sharpshooter was Confederate Lieutenant General Richard Ewell, who was atop his horse when a long-range Yankee slug slammed into his leg at the Second Battle of Winchester on 15 June 1863. Happily observing the result, Ewell quipped to Brigadier General John Gordon, "It don't hurt much to be shot in a wooden leg!" You see, the eccentric Ewell had lost that leg at the Second Bull Run.

Closer Calls

Quite a number of generals from both sides were not so fortunate. Singled out by sharpshooters due to their uniforms or mounts or actions, they were wounded but lived. The least injured of them was Brigadier General John Barry, a Confederate officer hit by a sharpshooter at Deep Bottom, Virginia, on 27 July 1864, resulting in the amputation of two fingers of his right hand.

Union General Walter Gresham was shot in the knee by a Rebel sharpshooter near Atlanta on 20 July 1864. Surviving his wound, he was discharged but went on to become U.S. Postmaster General under President Chester A. Arthur.

Also during the Atlanta Campaign, Union Brigadier General August Willich, "while observing the enemy from the parapet of the Thirty-Fifth Illinois," was severely wounded by a sharpshooter, ending his military career.

Union Brigadier General Francis Vinton, commanding the 3rd Brigade of the 2nd Division, was struck down by a Confederate sharpshooter at Fredericksburg. He, too, did not return to active duty.

At Chattanooga, Tennessee, Union Major General John Palmer, a division commander, paused to look through the opening on a rampart and instantly was knocked down by a sharpshooter's slug and seriously wounded.

Union Brigadier General Albert L. Lee, commanding the 1st Brigade of Brigadier General Peter J. Osterhaus' division, was hit in the face and severely wounded by a Rebel sharpshooter at Vicksburg.

At Atlanta, two Union generals were wounded in two days. Brigadier General Joseph Lightburn received a serious head wound from a Rebel sharpshooter on 19 August 1864. Just two days earlier, Major General Grenville Dodge, commanding the Union's XVI Corps, was badly wounded by a sharpshooter. Recovering, Dodge became a wealthy postwar railroad executive and one of the founders of the General Mills Corporation.

In the fall of 1863, at the Battle of the Wauhatchie, Union Brigadier General George Sears Greene was badly wounded by a sharpshooter whose bullet "entered at the lower left corner of his nose, and passed diagonally across his mouth, badly breaking his upper jaw and tearing out through his right cheek." The son of Revolutionary War General Nathaniel Greene, by 1892 he was the oldest surviving Union Army general and the oldest living West Point graduate. Suffering from his wound and in need of a pension for his family, he was enabled by a special act of Congress to take the oath of office at age 93 as a first lieutenant, his highest permanent rank, and retire the same day. He lived another five years. General Greene was the oldest first lieutenant in the history of the U.S. Army.

The saddest case I came upon of a wounded general is that of Brigadier General Patrick Robert Guiney, shot in the head by a Rebel sharpshooter on 5 May 1864 during the Battle of the Wilderness. Discharged due to disability, he attempted to continue his legal practice, but his permanent injury precluded him from pleading at trial. Sustained by sheer will, after a dozen years of therapy and suffering, he was found one morning kneeling beside a tree in a Boston park, dead at last from his terrible wound.

Colonel William R. Marshall, commanding the 7th Minnesota Regiment, survived a serious sharpshooter wound to become his state's governor.

Fighting Chaplins

Chaplain Lorenzo Barber, who ministered to the men of the 2nd U.S. Sharpshooter Regiment, arrived at the unit's 1861 tryouts like any other recruit—with a heavy-barreled target rifle. Earning his membership by shooting skill—and acclaimed as "one of the best shots in the army"— Chaplain Barber both serviced the sharpshooter's souls and dispensed well-aimed fire at the enemy.

Nicknamed "the Fighting Parson," he "had his telescope rifle sights marked for every 50 yards," and could be counted on to give the correct range to any distant target. Sharing the hazards of his countrymen, at Chancellorsville he engaged Rebel soldiers of the 23rd Georgia and found no contradiction with his religious beliefs. As one Berdan Sharpshooter put it, "His *faith* was in the 'Sword of the Lord and of Gideon,' but his best work was put in with a twenty-pound telescopic rifle which he used with wonderful effect." Sharpshooter Wyman S. White explained, "Chaplain Barber shot as he prayed, or in other words he helped to answer his own prayers by doing all he could to put down the rebellion."

By August 1864, so thin were sharpshooter officer ranks that Chaplain Barber had become the Army of the Potomac's Chief of Sharpshooters. Severely wounded that year, he recovered at his home in Troy, New York, only to die later in a tragic firearms accident.

Chaplain Lorenzo Barber, "the Fighting Parson" of the 2nd U.S. Sharpshooter Regiment.

The Confederacy had somewhat of a counterpart to Chaplain Barber, a Baptist Minister, Isaac Taylor Tichenor. A Kentucky native who had preached and had congregations across the South, in 1861 Reverend Tichenor was chaplain of the 17th Alabama Regiment. Like Barber, he both preached to the soldiers and fought alongside them, acquiring a reputation as a keen-eyed sharpshooter. At the Battle of Shiloh he rallied the regiment's wavering lines and helped save the day. For part of 1862, Reverend Tichenor served similarly with General Braxton Bragg's army, then went back to civilian religious duties.

Other chaplains took up both the cross and the rifle. Reverend Arthur Buckminster Fuller, an 1843 Harvard graduate, volunteered to be chaplain of the 16th Massachusetts Regiment. Discharged on 10 December 1863 due to ill health, he could not leave his brethren, for the following day was the Battle of Antietam. Accompanying his regiment, rifle in hand, he fought his way through the town—one of the war's few true urban fights—but was shot by a Rebel sharpshooter and died in front of a grocery store on Caroline Street.

The Reverend Francis Eugene Butler, a Princeton graduate with a congregation in Paterson, New Jersey, joined the 25th New Jersey Regiment as the unit chaplain. On 4 May 1863, "learning that some men of the Connecticut regiment on the right were suffering and in need of surgical assistance, he went to their relief and was shot by a sharpshooter and died the next day."

The Reverend Daniel Foster, a Dartmouth graduate and staunch abolitionist, in 1854 was chaplain of the Massachusetts House of Representatives. In 1857 he was elected to the Kansas House of Representatives to keep that state from becoming a haven of slavery. In August 1862, Reverend Foster went to war as chaplain of the 33rd Massachusetts Volunteers, but that was not enough for the activist minister. Commissioned a captain in the 37th U.S. Colored Troops, he went into direct combat and was killed by a Confederate sharpshooter at the Battle of Chapin's Bluff on 30 September 1864. An eyewitness reported that Reverend Foster "made a valiant but unsuccessful effort to turn himself around, so that he could make good on his vow to die facing the enemy." He was buried in West Newbury, Massachusetts, at the Pleasant Street Cemetery.

The Gettysburg monument to the 1st Company, Andrews Sharpshooters, depicts a soldier firing a "telescope rifle."

This monument to Michigan men belonging to Berdan's Sharpshooters stands on the west slope of Little Round Top, where they fought.

Silhouetted against the sky, this life-size statue of Major General Gouverneur Warren stands atop Little Round Top, where he was shot by a Rebel sharpshooter.

immediately killed or fled for their lives. "The men soon complained of having their arms and shoulders very much bruised by the continual kicking of the muskets," Blackford reported, "but still there could be no rest for them."

As Union counterfire struck the houses, the sharpshooters scurried from house to house through holes cut into intervening walls. They piled beds, furniture, and mattresses to give them as much protection as possible. Soon the rooms stank of black powder, and the heat grew so oppressive that they stripped to the waist. "I fired

84 rounds with careful aim into their midst, one gun cooling while the other was in use," said one sharpshooter. "My shoulder pad became so sore that I was obliged to rest."

Among the assaulting Confederate troops were sharpshooters who took a toll, as well. Union General John Gibbon, commanding II Corps, was knocked down and seriously wounded, he thought, by a sharpshooter. Many other Union officers fell, and in all the confusion no one could say who had fired such deadly projectiles.

That morning of 3 July, several Union sharpshooter units had reinforced the center of the line. The 2nd U.S. Sharpshooter Regiment placed its marksmen among the varied regiments holding Cemetery Ridge, while the 1st Company of Andrews Sharpshooters were in Ziegler's Grove, firing their telescope rifles at the Rebel sharpshooters in Gettysburg. Captain Emerson Bicknell of the Andrews Sharpshooters wrote, "I gathered a few men about me on [Cemetery] ridge and when the pressure upon our lines was at their height, picked off two or three mounted officers, who were pressing their men against our line just to the left of my position." As quickly as they could reload, alongside thousands of infantrymen, Union sharpshooters poured on well-aimed rifle fire.

The mass Confederate assault, known forever as Pickett's Charge, went on despite the continuous pummeling of cannon and rifle fire, swept up to the Union lines, then faltered, flickered, and finally ignominiously died. It was over. In three days, Lee's army had lost 27,000 men killed or wounded, slightly more than the Union's estimated 23,000 casualties. But the South's logistical cupboard was nearly bare, and her manpower pool almost spent, while the North's losses were serious but replaceable.

Among the dozens of key decisions and decisive actions that tipped the scales at Gettysburg, it is difficult to claim that any event or unit singularly turned the tide. Yet, the delay of Longstreet's forces on 2 July—accomplished by Berdan's Sharpshooters—and the fight for Little Round Top—which involved both Union and Confederate marksmen—are among those key events, and had they gone the other way, the outcome might well have been reversed. The death of General Reynolds by a Rebel sharpshooter markedly influenced the first day's fighting and led to Union forces falling back on Gettysburg's more favorable terrain—for worse or, as it turned out, for better.

Ironically, the most impressive Confederate sharpshooting performance at Gettysburg—the catastrophic decapitation of senior Union officers on Little Round Top—had little effect on Federal forces holding that critical terrain. Why? Despite the sudden losses, the Union troops already had been positioned, and they understood their mission: "Shoot anyone who comes your way." Had Rebel sharpshooters eliminated the same leaders a half-hour earlier—before they'd assessed the situation, made

Major General John Gibbon, commanding the Union's II Corps, lies wounded during Pickett's Charge, shot by a sharpshooter.

key decisions, and positioned their forces—the result quite likely would have been reversed, demonstrating that it was not just *which* leader was shot, but *when*.

On the very day of victory at Gettysburg, 4 July 1863, victory was achieved as well at Vicksburg, and here the sharpshooter contribution was at least as great.

CHAPTER EIGHT

Vicksburg to the Bitter End

B y the spring of 1863, there was no more strategic position in the western theater than Vicksburg, Mississippi. Located on a bluff overlooking the Mississippi River, halfway between Memphis and New Orleans, Vicksburg was the final Confederate bastion on that great waterway. Capture Vicksburg, General Ulysses S. Grant knew, and the Confederacy would be cut in half, its eastern armies separated from critical supplies in Texas, Arkansas, and Louisiana.

Grant's campaign began in early May, isolating the city and its high ground by

Miles of elaborate breastworks surrounded Vicksburg and (here) Petersburg, but even peeking over the top was risking one's life.

defeating Confederate armies deeper in Mississippi. After the Rebels easily repulsed a hasty Union assault on Vicksburg on 19 May, Grant prepared a deliberate attack, launched on 22 May.

This attack was heavily supported by sharpshooters, their fire especially focused on artillery crews. A captured Rebel artillery officer told the *New York Herald* that he had "seven men killed in succession while trying to sight one piece of artillery." Another Confederate officer, Major J.G. Devereux, reported, "No [artillery] piece could be served longer than ten minutes," due to intense Union sharpshooter fire.

Confederate sharpshooters were no less engaged. Advancing with his troops, Union Colonel W.M. Stone paused to speak with Lieutenant Colonel C.W. Dunlap, "when I was shot in the arm by a sharpshooter." A second later, a sharpshooter's bullet killed Colonel Dunlap, acting commander of the 21st Iowa Regiment. Not far away, a Union brigade commander, Colonel George B. Boomer, paused during the assault, and, although he minimized his size by lying prone, a well-place Rebel sharpshooter's bullet struck and killed him.

So intense was the fire that two Union regimental colors, abandoned a scant 10 feet from the Rebel works, fluttered in the wind unmolested all day; any attempt to seize them brought instant death.

The 22 May assault having failed, Grant's forces settled into a protracted siege. While Confederate Major General John Pemberton's 30,000 men defended 9 miles of trenches and hilltop strongpoints, Grant's 50,000 men slowly

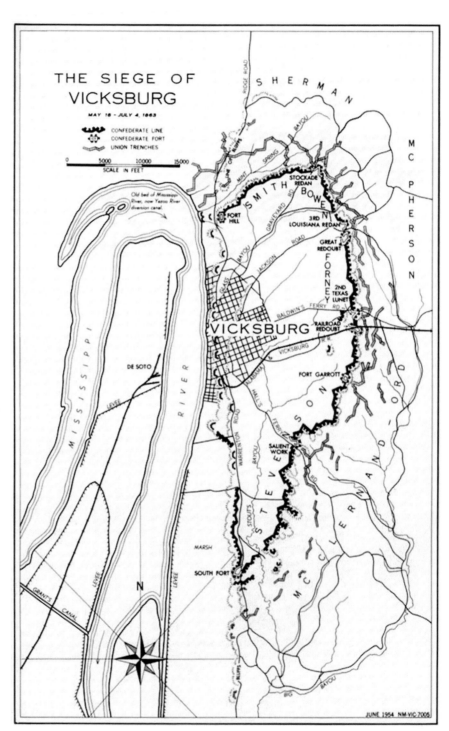

Nine miles of trenches and strong points ringed the doomed river town of Vicksburg.

The Psychological Effect

At crucial moments, the support of friendly sharpshooters could boost morale. Spirits soared in McGowan's Confederate Brigade, for example, after its men had failed in an attack and fallen back feeling defeated, only to hear their sharpshooters take on the Yankee infantry. "The familiar cry of our deadly rifles, reverberating through the forests, fell upon the ears of our comrades of the main line like vesper music at the close of the day," wrote a McGowan sharpshooter, "and contributed materially to the restoration of order."

Usually, however, it was enemy sharpshooters who affected morale, and rarely in a positive way. Beyond their direct military effect and the number of casualties they inflicted, the common soldier found sharpshooters a lethal irritation that he could not fight, a constant, unseen threat that hovered out there, beyond his vision and beyond the range of his rifle.

Professor D.H. Mahan, a West Point instructor, believed "nothing is more dreaded by troops generally than this lurking and often invisible foe, whose whereabouts is only divined by the destruction he deals around him."

Confederate Brigadier General W.N. Pendleton called Union sharpshooters "an evil not slightly trying" for their lethal efficiency at picking off his artillerymen at the Battle of Sharpsburg. His gun crews could do nothing, Pendleton knew, because the terrain left them vulnerable to long-range fire "by the enemy's effective rifles."

Caught in a similar situation, Captain James Wood of the 37th Virginia Infantry Regiment complained that "well posted sharpshooters with guns of longer range than our's were very annoying and damaging." Fatalistically, he reported, "Our men were thus picked off here and there with remarkable regularity. In places of such danger good fortune seemed to follow some and bad fortune others."

Rebel infantryman Albert R. Greene, his morale sapped, described how at Lookout Mountain, Tennessee, he and his comrades suffered the misery of unending sharpshooter fire in addition to "cold, fatigue and hunger. . . . It seemed as if our blood was cold and the last spark of vitality frozen within us. At the slightest attempt to make a fire the sharpshooters on the palisades would open on us, and all attempts were forbidden."

This psychological effect grew considerably worse during protracted sieges, like Vicksburg and Petersburg, where well-positioned sharpshooters on both sides harvested lives anonymously, day and night, for weeks at a time. As Winslow Homer so well captured in the accompanying painting, the stress of this unrelenting, unseen danger could drive otherwise disciplined men to madness.

"*INVITING THE SHOT.*" Winslow Homer's haunting depiction of a crazed Confederate soldier, driven mad by constant fire, steps atop a parapet, daring Union sharpshooters to kill him. (Courtesy of Virginia Museum of Fine Arts.)

advanced a labyrinth of trenches forward. Like a python ever tightening its grip, Union engineers' trenches squeezed closer and closer to Confederate positions, covered all along the way by precision sharpshooter fire.

Requiring every bit as much exactness as long-range shooting, this close-range sharpshooting focused at tiny, often fleeting targets as little as 60 yards away. As General Grant wrote, "Their infantry was kept down by our sharpshooters, who were always on alert and ready to fire whenever it showed itself above the Rebel works."

Union Lieutenant Colonel Harrison Strong, an expert marksman, tries his hand at sharpshooting.

"As the trenches progressed," wrote Union Brigadier General Mortimer Leggett, "I advanced my sharpshooters, thus protecting as much as possible those at work on the trenches." And with each trench extension, Leggett explained, "as soon as possible loop-holed timber was placed upon the works for the sharpshooters." He singled out Lieutenant J.W. Miller of the 54th Ohio for "courage and physical endurance" in leading his brigade sharpshooters.

Sharpshooter C.L. Ruggles of the 20th Ohio took on several Confederate artillery crews and achieved sufficient fame that General Grant personally presented him with a new rifle. Wrote another 20th Ohio soldier, "It is shoot, shoot, dodge, dodge from morning to night, without cessation, except when we sleep." To allow sharpshooters to fire deeper into Confederate positions, Union engineers erected a tall shooting platform, known as "Coonskin Tower." Other sharpshooters, according to an Iowa veteran, would dig "rat holes on the outer side of the parapet and fire incessantly."

As the siege continued, a few freelance sharpshooters tried their hand at it. Notable among them was Lieutenant Colonel Harrison Strong, an officer on General James B. McPherson's staff and an expert marksman. He put an artillery crew out of action and then shot dead a Rebel sharpshooter he detected low-crawling between the trenches.

The Confederate defenders, meanwhile, were doing their best to stave off the approaching Yankee trenches. "To impede the progress of the enemy's work as much as possible," reported a Confederate brigade commander, "I have directed the sharpshooting of my men there to be increased, having one

"I am the only officer left in the company."

No account of Vicksburg so well captures the effect of relentless sharpshooter fire as the diary of Captain W.L. Faulk, commander of Company B, 38th Mississippi Infantry. Facing incessant casualties and few means to counter the enemy's sharpshooters, Faulk documented his unit's declining strength and will during the 43-day siege in these diary extracts.

May 20   10 o'clock. Adjutant Ward wounded in both legs by a sharpshooter . . . have been under heavy fire from the sharpshooters. . . . Five or six men in the regiment wounded and one killed from Co. I. . . . One man from my company slightly wounded—D.Y. Legust. I forgot to mention yesterday the wounding of Lieut. Lainhart, said to be mortal.

May 23   All very quiet along our lines last night and up to present time . . . except some sharpshooting. We are called upon to regret the loss of Capt. Gravis. He was killed early this morning by a sharpshooter.

May 24   Sharpshooting and artillery fire all day.

May 25   Nothing heard but the firing of sharpshooters. . . . One man killed in Co. D by a sharpshooter this morning. . . . We have been permitted to come from the ditches and walk about and relieved from the continuous firing of the sharpshooters and cannon . . .

May 26   All quiet except occasional firing by cannon and continuous sharpshooting. I regret the wounding of one of my best men (Louis Segrest) who was shot just below the knee, causing a fracture of one of the bones; also one man from Co. E wounded at the spring while getting water. . . . Nine days we have been confined to the ditches, only permitted to walk around after dark.

May 27   Another beautiful morning . . . and still the popping of guns from sharpshooters continues and occasional peals from the enemy's cannons . . . . I am the only officer left in the company. 6 o'clock. . . . The incessant sharpshooting continues.

May 28   The enemy still continue their shelling and sharpshooting.

May 30   [T]his morning the sharpshooters are popping away as usual . . .

June 2   All quiet again this morning except the usual sharpshooting and occasional cannonading.

June 6   One man from Co. I shot in the finger by a sharpshooter last night.

June 8   The enemy have been quiet for several days past. The sharpshooters keep up a continual firing, for what reason they alone know for they can see nothing to shoot at.

June 11   Very heavy sharpshooting yesterday and this morning.

June 13   The same old routine of shelling and sharpshooting still continues.

June 14   This is a beautiful morning and were it not for the incessant firing of the sharpshooters all would be perfectly quiet as it should be on this [Sabbath] day.

June 17   One man killed by a sharpshooter in Co. I.

June 18   One man from Co. K killed by sharpshooters.

June 21   W.T. Adair of my company was wounded by a sharpshooter, I am afraid badly.

June 24   Another man killed in our regiment today from Company I.

June 25   God in his wisdom has seen fit to take from us one of our best soldiers (Aleck Cameron). He was good in all that constitutes a soldier—brave, noble, and true—one who never shrank from danger or murmured at duty—always ready to encourage the men under the greatest hardships and privations. He was shot by a sharpshooter in the left eye whilst looking over the parapet last night about 9 o'clock. His death has cast a gloom over our little company, and it will be long before we can realize that Aleck is no more . . . another man in Co. C wounded by sharpshooters.

June 26   Very heavy sharpshooting in front of our position last night. . . . Another man killed in Co. I today by sharpshooters. We are losing men very rapidly.

Multiply the experience of Captain Faulk's company by 100 or more, and you can begin to grasp the deadly effect of sharpshooters on all the Confederate infantry companies defending the 9-mile Vicksburg perimeter.

"Shooting for Epaulets"

Sharpshooters on both sides opportunistically "shot for the epaulets"—that is, they attempted to shoot senior officers, distinguished traditionally by gold shoulder boards with hanging tassels. Each time a sharpshooter killed or seriously wounded a senior leader, his loss potentially disrupted command and coordination, particularly if that officer was directing an attack. When popular leaders fell, morale suffered, too. Consider, then, the effect of losing all these leaders at critical times and places—keeping in mind that this is an incomplete representation gleaned from various regimental and divisional histories.

Killed by a sharpshooter at Chickamauga, Union Colonel Hans Christian Heg. Norwegian by birth, Heg previously had commanded the 15th Wisconsin Volunteer Infantry.

21 June 1861	Union Navy **Commander James H. Ward**, commander, Potomac Flotilla, shot dead by a Confederate sharpshooter while aboard the USS *Thomas Freeborn*, the first naval officer to die in the Civil War.
13 July 1861	CSA **Brigadier General Robert S. Garnett**, a brigade commander at Corrick's Ford, Virginia, shot dead by a Union sharpshooter, the first general officer to die in the Civil War.
10 August 1861	Union **Brigadier General Nathaniel Lyon**, commander of Northern forces at the Battle of Wilson's Creek, Missouri, killed by a Confederate sharpshooter.
10 September 1861	CSA **Lieutenant Colonel John Washington**, staff officer to General Robert E. Lee, killed by Union sharpshooter at Cheat Mountain, West Virginia.
21 October 1861	Union **Colonel James Baker**, commanding a brigade-size diversionary force, killed by a Confederate sharpshooter at Balls Bluff, Virginia.
15 February 1862	CSA **Lieutenant Colonel Alfred Robb**, regimental executive officer, shot dead by a Union sharpshooter at Fort Donelson, Tennessee.
7 March 1862	CSA **Brigadier General Ben McCulloch**, commander of a Confederate brigade, shot dead by a Union sharpshooter at Elkhorn Tavern, Arkansas.
22 March 1862	Union **Colonel William Murray**, commander, 84th Pennsylvania Volunteer Infantry, killed by a Confederate sharpshooter at Kernstown, Virginia.
14 September 1862	Union **Major General Jesse Reno**, commander, IX Corps, shot dead by Confederate sharpshooter at Fox's Gap, Maryland.
17 September 1862	Union **Major General Joseph K.F. Mansfield**, commander, XII Corps, killed by a Confederate sharpshooter at Antietam Creek, Maryland.
17 September 1862	CSA **Brigadier General Lawrence O'Bryan Branch**, a brigade commander in Hill's Division, killed by a Union sharpshooter at Antietam Creek, Maryland.
31 December 1862	Union **Colonel Leander Stem**, commander of the 101st Ohio Infantry Regiment, shot dead by a Confederate sharpshooter, Stones River, Tennessee.
3 May 1863	Union **Colonel Amor McKnight**, commander, 105th Pennsylvania Volunteer Infantry, killed by a Confederate sharpshooter at Chancellorsville, Virginia.
3 May 1863	Union **Colonel Henry J. Stainrook**, commander, 2nd Brigade, 2nd Division, "instantly killed" by Confederate sharpshooter at Chancellorsville, Virginia.
3 May 1863	CSA **Colonel Thomas J. Purdie**, commander, 18th North Carolina Regiment, killed by a Union sharpshooter at Chancellorsville, Virginia. (Possibly "suicide by sharpshooter," for one day earlier Purdie had ordered his troops to open fire, accidentally killing the irreplaceable General Thomas "Stonewall" Jackson.)
4 May 1863	Union **Major General Amiel W. Whipple**, division commander, shot dead by a Confederate sharpshooter, Chancellorsville, Virginia.
22 May 1863	Union **Lieutenant Colonel C.W. Dunlap**, acting commander, 21st Iowa Regiment, killed by Confederate sharpshooter, Vicksburg, Mississippi.
22 May 1863	Union **Colonel George Boomer**, commander, 22nd Missouri Volunteers, killed by a Confederate sharpshooter at Vicksburg, Mississippi.

23 May 1863	Union **Colonel John Richter Jones**, commander, 58th Pennsylvania Volunteer Infantry, killed by a Confederate sharpshooter near Batchelders Creek, North Carolina.
27 May 1863	Union **Colonel David Cowles**, commander, 128th Regiment, New York Volunteers, killed by a Confederate sharpshooter at Port Hudson, Mississippi.
17 June 1863	CSA **Brigadier General Isham Garrott**, a brigade commander, shot dead by a Union sharpshooter at Vicksburg, Mississippi.
24 June 1863	CSA **Colonel Eugene Erwin**, commander, 6th Missouri Infantry Regiment, shot dead by a Union sharpshooter at Vicksburg, Mississippi.
27 June 1863	CSA **Brigadier General Martin Edward Green**, commander, 2nd Brigade, Bowen's Division, killed by a Union sharpshooter, Vicksburg, Mississippi.
30 June 1863	CSA **Colonel James W. Starnes**, commander, 4th Tennessee Cavalry Regiment, shot dead by a Union sharpshooter near Tullahoma, Tennessee.
1 July 1863	Union **General John F. Reynolds**, commander, forward element, Army of the Potomac (I, II, IX Corps), killed by Confederate sharpshooter, Gettysburg.
1 July 1863	Union **Lieutenant Colonel Douglas Fowler**, commander, 17th Connecticut Regiment, killed by suspected Confederate sharpshooter, Gettysburg.
2 July 1863	Union **Colonel Edward Cross**, commander of a Union brigade, killed by a Confederate sharpshooter, Gettysburg.
2 July 1863	CSA **Lieutenant Colonel William Shepherd**, commander, 2nd Georgia Infantry Regiment, mortally wounded by a suspected Union sharpshooter, Gettysburg.
2 July 1863	CSA **Brigadier General William Barksdale**, brigade commander, believed killed by a Union sharpshooter, Gettysburg.
2 July 1863	Union **Colonel Charles F. Taylor**, commander, 1st Pennsylvania Rifle Regiment, killed by a Confederate sharpshooter, Gettysburg.
3 July 1863	Union **Brigadier General Stephen Weed**, commander, 3rd Brigade, 2nd Division, killed by a Confederate sharpshooter, Gettysburg.
3 July 1863	Union **Brigadier General Strong Vincent**, commander, 3rd Brigade, 1st Division, mortally wounded by a Confederate sharpshooter, Gettysburg.
3 July 1863	Union **Colonel Patrick O'Rourke**, commander, 140th New York Infantry, shot dead by a Confederate sharpshooter, Gettysburg.
18 July 1863	Union **Colonel John Toland**, commander, 34th Ohio Volunteer Infantry Regiment, killed by Confederate sharpshooter, Wytheveille, Virginia.
19 September 1863	Union **Colonel Hans Christian Heg**, commander, 3rd Brigade, 1st Division, mortally wounded by a Confederate sharpshooter at Chickamauga, Georgia.
20 September 1863	Union **Colonel Edward King**, commander, 2nd Brigade, 4th Division, killed by a Confederate sharpshooter at Chickamauga, Georgia.
20 September 1863	Union **Brigadier General William Lytle**, commander, 1st Brigade, 3rd Division, killed by a Confederate sharpshooter at Chickamauga, Georgia.
19 November 1863	Union **Major General William P. Sanders**, division commander, shot dead by Confederate sharpshooter, Knoxville, Tennessee.
24 November 1863	Union **Colonel Gilbert Elliott**, commander, 102nd New York Volunteers, shot dead by a Confederate sharpshooter at Lookout Mountain, Tennessee.
8 April 1864	Union **Lieutenant Colonel Lysander Webb**, commander, 77th Illinois Volunteer Infantry Regiment, shot dead by a Confederate sharpshooter at Mansfield, Louisiana.
6 May 1864	CSA **Lieutenant Colonel Francis Boone**, executive officer, 26th Mississippi Regiment, killed by Union sharpshooter at The Wilderness.
9 May 1864	Union **Major General John Sedgwick**, commander, VI Corps, killed instantly by a Confederate sharpshooter, Spotsylvania, Virginia, after uttering the ironic last words, "Why, they couldn't hit an elephant at this dist . . . "
10 May 1864	Union **Brigadier General Thomas Stevenson**, division commander, killed by a Confederate sharpshooter, Spotsylvania.
25 May 1864	CSA **Colonel Merry Harris**, commander, 12th Mississippi Infantry Regiment, mortally wounded by Union sharpshooter, Cold Harbor, Virginia.

▶

25 May 1864	CSA **Colonel Amos Riley**, commander, 4th Missouri Regiment, shot and killed by Union sharpshooter at New Hope Church, Georgia.
27 May 1864	Union **Major James Hampson**, executive officer, 120th Ohio Infantry Regiment, killed by a Confederate sharpshooter, near Chickamauga, Georgia.
28 May 1864	Union **Colonel L.O. Morris**, commander, 7th New York Heavy Artillery Regiment, killed by a Confederate sharpshooter at Cold Harbor, Virginia.
31 May 1864	CSA **Colonel J.T. Brown**, Assistant Commander of Artillery, Army of Northern Virginia, killed by a Union sharpshooter, Wilderness, Virginia.
2 June 1864	CSA **Brigadier General George P. Doles**, brigade commander, killed by a Union sharpshooter, near Bethesda Church, Virginia.
3 June 1864	Union **Major Joseph Gilmour**, commander, Pennsylvania 48th Regiment, killed by Confederate sharpshooter near Cold Harbor, Virginia.
9 June 1864	Union **Colonel Thomas F. Burpee**, commander, Infantry Regiment, Volunteer Infantry Regiment, mortally wounded by a Confederate sharpshooter at Cold Harbor, Virginia.

A retired judge, Colonel John Richter Jones raised and led the 58th Pennsylvania Volunteer Infantry Regiment until he was killed by a Confederate sharpshooter. (Courtesy of James Di Risio.)

23 June 1864	Union **Colonel Frederick Bartleson**, commander, 100th Illinois Infantry Regiment, killed by a Confederate sharpshooter at (Kennesaw Mountain, Georgia.
23 June 1864	Union **Colonel William Blaisdell**, brigade commander, killed by a Confederate sharpshooter, Petersburg, Virginia.
21 July 1864	CSA **Colonel Samuel Adams**, commander, 33rd Alabama Regiment, "instantly killed" by a Union sharpshooter at Kennesaw Mountain, Georgia.
22 July 1864	CSA **Major General William H.T. Walker**, division commander, killed by a Union sharpshooter near Atlanta, Georgia.
24 July 1864	Union **Brigadier General James Mulligan**, commander, 3rd Division, shot dead by a Confederate sharpshooter at Kernstown, Virginia.
18 August 1864	Union **Colonel Daniel Chaplin**, commander, 1st Maine Heavy Artillery, mortally wounded by a Confederate sharpshooter at Deep Bottom, Virginia.
6 February 1865	CSA **Brigadier General John Pegram**, division commander, killed by a Union sharpshooter, Hatcher's Run, Virginia.
8 April 1865	Union **Major Shesh B. Howe**, executive officer, 1st West Virginia Cavalry, killed by a Confederate sharpshooter the night before Lee's surrender, at Appomattox, Virginia.
8 April 1865	Union **Brigadier General Thomas Smyth**, commander, 3rd Division, II Corps, mortally wounded by a Confederate sharpshooter the day before Lee surrendered, near Appomattox Courthouse, the last Union general to die in the war.
16 April 1865	CSA **Brigadier General Robert C. Tyler**, commander, Fort Tyler, killed by a Union sharpshooter a full week after Lee's surrender, the last general of either side to die in the Civil War, at West Point, Georgia.

CSA Brigadier General Isham Garrott. On 17 June 1863 he was killed while attempting to shoot a Union sharpshooter.

Confederate Brigadier General Martin Edward Green was killed by a Union sharpshooter at Vicksburg, 27 June 1863, after saying, "A bullet has not yet been molded that will kill me."

sharpshooter every 8 or 9 yards in the rifle pits, to fire whenever they see anything to shoot at."

Rebel ranks included some fine marksmen, among them a one-eyed man who fired a Belgian-made rifle. Belonging to the 30th Alabama and known as that state's best marksman, he was named Elliott, though he had the nickname of "Old One-Eye." According to the *Charleston Mercury*, Elliott was reputed to have made several kills at 1,000 yards, and, it was claimed, he once shot two Union officers with a single bullet.

For their part, Union sharpshooters, too, were taking a bloody toll of Confederate forces.

"Our entire line became subject to murderous fire," reported CSA Brigadier General Louis Hebert, "and nearly every cannon on my line was in time either dismounted or otherwise injured." General Pemberton informed his superior, Lieutenant General Joseph Johnston, that Union sharpshooters were shooting his officers and men "whenever they showed themselves." Another Rebel officer observed, "The sharpshooters are extremely vigilant and are within 60 or 70 yards, excellently covered." In particular, Confederate soldiers dreaded a spot they called "the Dead Hole," from which hidden Yankee sharpshooters had shot 17 men.

Rebel losses reached high into their command level. The 6th Missouri Regimental commander, Colonel Eugene Erwin—grandson of the great orator Henry Clay—"sprang on the parapet to lead a charge against the enemy," but he was "shot and instantly killed" by a single, well-placed shot.

The highest-ranking Vicksburg targets felled by Union sharpshooters were Brigadier Generals Isham Garrott on 17 June and Martin Edward Green 10 days later. Annoyed by the continual sharpshooter fire, Garrott died while attempting to shoot a Union sharpshooter. Green, commander of the 2nd Brigade in Brigadier

General John S. Bowen's division, only moments before his fatal wound had shrugged off warnings of sharpshooters by saying, "A bullet has not yet been molded that will kill me."

After suffering 42 days of relentless sharpshooter and artillery fire—his army famished and half his men killed, wounded, or sick—Pemberton had no choice but to surrender. His men laid down their arms the same day that Lee's defeated army withdrew from Gettysburg.

THE CLOSING DAYS

Despite the Confederacy's strategic reversals at Gettysburg and Vicksburg, the war dragged on another 21 months, and, every day, every step of the way, sharpshooters played a role and took their toll. Particularly, their precision fire came to the fore during the siege of Petersburg where, repeating their deadly effect at Vicksburg, they struck down any man who lifted his head above the parapets—Union or Confederate. And during the Atlanta Campaign of 1864, Rebel sharpshooters fighting on familiar ground proved especially adept at picking off Union officers.

Despite all the lessons learned and combat achievements, the Union Army's highest levels of command still did not appreciate the value and role of sharpshooters. In late 1864, when many Berdan Sharpshooters' enlistments expired, the War Department did not replace them nor seek new recruits—perhaps out of resentment for their

Michigan sharpshooter Sidney Haight (right), here with his brother James, was awarded the Medal of Honor for gallantry during the Petersburg siege.

elite status—instead gradually drawing down the unit and transferring the remaining men to other regiments. On 25 February 1865, just 42 days before Lee's surrender, "much to the disgust of officers and men," the War Department officially disbanded the 1st and 2nd U.S. Sharpshooter Regiments. Promoted to brigadier general, Hiram Berdan was discharged.

The Final Casualties

The Civil War's final losses among general officers were inflicted by the precision shots of sharpshooters. Union Brigadier General Thomas A. Smyth, a courageous leader, had enlisted in the war's opening days and risen by merit through the ranks of the 1st Delaware Regiment. By the Battle of Gettysburg, Smyth wore a star and commanded an infantry brigade. Just two days before Lee's surrender at Appomattox, a few miles away, Smyth, then commanding the 3rd Division, II Corps, rode his unit's skirmish line. Spotted by a Confederate sharpshooter, one well-placed shot struck him in the neck, paralyzing him. Two days later he died, the last Union general to perish in the war.

Equally tragic was the loss of Confederate Brigadier General Robert C. Tyler, like Smyth, a self-made man who had enlisted as a private in 1861. By the Battle of Shiloh he commanded the 15th Tennessee Regiment; then, at Missionary Ridge, while capturing a Union cannon, he lost his left leg. On Easter Sunday, 16 April 1865, a week after Lee's Army of Northern Virginia had laid down its arms, General Tyler and 120 men made the Confederacy's last stand at West Point, Georgia, 30 miles north of Columbus. Defending a tiny earthen fort, Tyler's men held off a numerically superior Union cavalry force until just after noon. Then, according to Confederate Private Isham Stanley:

Brigadier General Thomas Smyth was the last Union general to die in the Civil War.

The Civil War's final fallen general, Confederate Brigadier General Robert C. Tyler, died in the conflict's last battle.

> "General Tyler deliberately walked in front of the wall . . . exposing his whole body to the enemy. When about midway he stopped, left-faced, which movement turned his whole front to the enemy. At that moment he fell, and never moved a muscle . . ."

From a facing house, a Union sharpshooter had fired a single shot.

With Tyler's death, his surrounded, outnumbered men lay down their arms. General Tyler was the last general on either side to die in the American Civil War.

On the Confederate side, sharpshooters fought on to the bitter end. As the defeated Lee fell back from Petersburg to Appomattox and inevitable surrender, sharpshooter commander Major Dunlop wrote:

> "I stood upon a stump on the hill to the eastward of the Federal column where the left wing of sharpshooters were contending with the Federal right, and great tears of overwhelming admiration flowed down my cheeks in streams, as I contemplated the grand courage of that glorious little band of unfaltering heroes, fighting to the very death for a cause already lost. I could hardly stand it."

Earlier, General William Hardee had called in his defeated sharpshooters and told them, "Had every man in our army been as effective as you, had they every one done as much execution as each of you, Sherman would not now have a man left."

Georgia sharpshooter Berry Benson and his surviving comrades did not form up with the others surrendering at Appomattox. They simply turned and walked toward home, their rifles still in their hands.

Bibliography

Baker, Ezekiel. *Remarks on Rifle Guns: Being the Result of Sixty Years' Practice and Observation, etc.* London: Joseph Mallett, 1835.

Baldwin, James J. III. *The Struck Eagle: A Biography of Brigadier General Micah Jenkins and a History of the Fifth South Carolina Volunteers and the Palmetto Sharpshooters.* Shippensburg, Penn.: Burd Street Press, 1996.

Barker, Lorenzo. *Birge's Western Sharpshooters in the Civil War, 1861–1865.* Huntington, W.V.: Blue Acorn Press, 1994 (reprint of 1905 edition).

Barnes, Frank C., and Ken Warner, eds. *Cartridges of the World* (6th ed.). Northbrook, Ill.: DBI Books, 1990.

Barron, Elwyn A., ed. *Deeds of Heroism and Bravery.* New York: Harper & Brothers, 1920.

Barrow, Charles Kelly, J.H. Segar, and R.B. Rosenburg, eds. *Forgotten Confederates: An Anthology About Black Southerners,* Atlanta: Southern Heritage Press, 1995.

Benedict, G.G. *Vermont in the Civil War: A History of the Part Taken by Vermont Soldiers and Sailors in the War for the Union.* Burlington, Vt.: The Free Press Association, 1888.

Benson, Susan Williams. *Barry Benson's Civil War Book: Memoirs of a Confederate Scout and Sharpshooter.* Athens, Ga.: University of Georgia Press, 1994.

Bosworth, N. *A Treatise on the Rifle, Pistol and Fowling-Piece.* Clinton Hall, N.Y.: J.S. Redfield, 1846.

Busk, Hans. *Hand-Book for Hythe: A Familiar Explanation of the Laws of Projectiles and an Introduction to the System of Musketry.* London: Southledge, Warne 7 Routledge, 1860.

Catton, Bruce. *The Army of the Potomac: Glory Road.* Garden City, N.Y.: Doubleday, 1953.

———. *The Army of the Potomac: Mr. Lincoln's Army.* Garden City, N.Y.: Doubleday, 1953.

———. *The Army of the Potomac: A Stillness at Appomattox.* Garden City, N.Y.: Doubleday, 1953.

———. *Grant Takes Command.* Boston: Little, Brown, 1968.

Chapman, John Ratcliffe. *Instructions to Young Marksmen in all that Relates to the Improved American Rifle.* New York: D. Appleton & Co., 1848.

Clemmer, Gregg S. *Valor in Gray: The Recipients of the Confederate Medal of Honor.* Staunton, Va.: Hearthside Publishing Co., 1996.

Coggins, Jack. *Arms and Equipment of the Civil War,* Garden City, N.Y.: Doubleday & Co., 1962.

The Diagram Group. *Weapons: An International Encyclopedia from 5000 B.C. to 2000 A.D.* New York: St. Martin's Press, 1990.

Dickinson, Jack L., ed. *Diary of a Confederate Sharpshooter: The Life of James Conrad Peters.* Charleston, W.V.: Pictorial Histories Publishing Co., 1997.

Dunlop, Major W.S. *Lee's Sharpshooters, or The Forefront of Battle.* Dayton, Ohio: Morningside, 1988 (reprint of 1899 edition).

Dupuy, Trevor N., Curt Johnson, and David L. Bongard, eds. *Harper Encyclopedia of Military Biography.* New York: HarperCollins, 1992.

Eggenberger, David. *A Dictionary of Battles.* New York: Thomas Y. Cromwell Co., 1967.

Faust, Patricia L., ed. *Historical Times Illustrated Encyclopedia of the Civil War,* New York: Harper Perennial, 1986.

Fletcher, William A. *Rebel Private: Front and Rear.* New York: Dutton, 1995.

Fox, Lieutenant Colonel William F. *Regimental Losses in the American Civil War.* Albany, N.Y.: Albany Publishing Co., 1889.

Greener, W.W. *Sharpshooting for War and Sport.* Prescott, Ariz.: Wolfe Publishing Co., 1995 (reprint of 1900 edition).

Guernsey, Alfred H., and Henry M. Alden. *Harper's Pictorial History of the Civil War.* Fairfax, Va.: Fairfax Press, 1866.

Hamley, Edward Bruce. *The Operations of War Explained and Illustrated.* Edinburgh and London: William Blackwood & Sons, 1869.

Hastings, William H. *Letters from a Sharpshooter: The Civil War Letters of Private William B. Greene, Co. G, 2nd United States Sharpshooters (Berdan's), Army of the Potomac.* Belleville, Wis.: Historic Publications, 1993.

Hauptman, Laurence M. *Between Two Fires: American Indians in the Civil War.* New York: The Free Press, 1995.

Herek, Raymond J. *These Men Have Seen Hard Service: The First Michigan Sharpshooters in the Civil War.* Detroit: Wayne State University Press, 1998.

Hunt, Harrison. *Heroes of the Civil War.* New York: Military Press, 1990.

Jones, Virgil Carrington. *Gray Ghosts and Rebel Raiders.* New York: Galahad Books, 1956.

Kinhard, Philip B., Philip B. Kinhard III, and Peter W. Kinhard. *Lincoln: An Illustrated Biography.* New York: Alfred Knopf, 1992.

Lippitt, Colonel Francis J. *A Treatise on the Tactical Use of the Three Arms: Infantry, Artillery, and Cavalry.* New York: D. Van Nostrand, 1865.

Lossing, Benson J. *Harpers' Popular Cyclopaedia of United States History from the Aboriginal Period, Vol. II.* New York: Harper & Brothers, 1893.

Mahon, John, and Romana Danysh. *Army Lineage Series: Infantry, Part I, Regular Army.* Washington, D.C.: Office of the Chief of Military History, U.S. Army, 1972.

Marcot, Roy M. *Civil War Chief of Sharpshooters: Hiram Berdan, Military Commander and Firearms Inventor.* Irvine, Calif.: Northwood Heritage Press, 1989.

McConnell, William F. *Remember Reno: A Biography of Major General Jesse Lee Reno.* Shippensburg, Penn.: White Mane Publishing Co., 1996.

Montgomery, George F., Jr. *Georgia Sharpshooter: The Civil War Diary and Letters of William Rhadamantuhus Montgomery, 1839–1906.* Macon, Ga.: Mercer University Press, 1997.

———. *War Through the Ages.* New York: Harper & Row, 1944.

Morrow, John Anderson. *The Confederate Whitworth Sharpshooters.* Atlanta: self-published, 1989.

Myatt, Frederick. *An Illustrated Encyclopedia of 19th Century Firearms.* New York: Random House, 1994.

National Rifle Association. *NRA Firearms Fact Book.* Washington, D.C.: NRA Books, 1989.

Norton, Oliver Willcox. *The Attack and Defense of Little Round Top, Gettysburg, July 2, 1863.* Gettysburg: Stan Clark Military Books, 1992 (reprint of 1913 edition).

O'Connor, Richard. *Wild Bill Hickok.* New York: Longmeadow Press, 1959.

Plaster, John L. *The Ultimate Sniper.* Boulder, Colo.: Paladin Press, 1993, 2006.

Pollard, E.A. *The Southern History of the War*. Fairfax, Va.: Fairfax Press, 1988 (reprint of 1879 edition).

Porter, General Horace. *Campaigning with Grant*. New York: Bonanza Books, 1961.

Ripley, Lieutenant Colonel William Y.W. *Vermont Riflemen in the War for the Union, 1861 to 1865: A History of Company F, First United States Sharpshooters*. Rutland, Vt.: Tuttle & Co., 1883.

Robertson, William G. *The Battle of Chickamauga*. Fort Washington, Penn.: Eastern National Park and Monument Association, 1995.

Rosa, Joseph G. *They Called Him Wild Bill: The Life and Adventures of James Butler Hickok*. Norman: University of Oklahoma Press, 1964.

Rywell, Martin. *Sharps Rifle: The Gun That Shaped American Destiny*. Union City, Tenn.: Pioneer Press, 1994.

Sawyer, Charles Winthrop. *Firearms in American History* (3 vols.). Boston: Cornhill Co., 1910.

Sharpe, Philip B. *The Rifle in America*. New York: Funk & Wagnalls Co., 1946.

Smith, W.H.B. *Small Arms of the World* (8th ed.). Harrisburg, Penn.: Stackpole Books, 1967.

State of Minnesota. *Minnesota in the Civil and Indian Wars, 1861–65, Volume II*. St. Paul: The Pioneer Press Co., 1899.

Stevens, Captain C.A. *Berdan's United States Sharpshooters in the Army of the Potomac, 1861–1865*. Dayton, Ohio: Morningside Bookshop, 1984 (reprint of 1892 edition).

Storrick, W.C. *Gettysburg: The Place, the Battles, the Outcome*. New York: Barnes & Noble Books, 1993.

Sword, Wiley. *Sharpshooter: Hiram Berdan, His Famous Shooters and Their Sharps Rifles*. Lincoln, R.I.: Andrew Mobray, Inc., 1988.

Trudeau, Noah Andre. *The Last Citadel: Petersburg, Virginia, June 1864–April 1865*. Baton Rouge: Louisiana State University Press, 1991.

———. *The Siege of Petersburg*. Fort Washington, Penn.: Eastern National Park and Monument Association, 1995.

United Confederate Veterans. *Confederate Veteran* (annual bound volumes). Nashville, Tenn.: 1898, 1899, 1900.

White, Russell C., ed. *The Civil War Diary of Wyman S. White: First Sergeant of Company F, 2nd United States Sharpshooter Regiment, 1861–1865*. Baltimore: Butternut & Blue, 1993.

Wyeth, John Allen, M.D. *The Life of General Nathan Bedford Forrest*. New York: Harper & Brothers, 1899.

Index

100th Illinois Infantry Regiment, 140
101st Ohio Infantry Regiment, 92, 138
102nd New York Volunteers, 93, 139
105th Pennsylvania Volunteer Infantry, 138
10th Massachusetts Battery, 89–90
11th Connecticut Regiment, 111
11th Pennsylvania Reserves, 101
102nd Pennsylvania Volunteer Infantry, 112
120th Ohio Infantry Regiment, 140
128th Regiment, New York Volunteers, 139
12th Mississippi Infantry Regiment, 139
12th West Virginia Infantry, 98
13th Illinois Infantry Regiment, 13
13th Indiana Volunteer Infantry, 12–13
13th Mississippi Infantry Regiment, 117
13th Virginia Infantry Regiment, 17
140th New York Infantry, 125, 139
14th Missouri Infantry Volunteers, 31
14th North Carolina Infantry, 34
150th Pennsylvania Regiment, 121
15th Tennessee Regiment, 143
15th Wisconsin Volunteer Infantry, 138
16th Illinois Cavalry, 101
16th Massachusetts Regiment, 128
16th South Carolina, 98, 103
17th Alabama Regiment, 128
17th Connecticut Regiment, 139
17th Maine Infantry, 12
17th Michigan Infantry, 95
17th Missouri Infantry Regiment, 117

18th Mississippi Infantry Regiment, 117
18th North Carolina Regiment, 138
19th Massachusetts Regiment, 117
1st Battalion, New York Sharpshooters, 60
1st Brigade, 3rd Division, 139
1st Delaware Regiment, 143
1st Maine Heavy Artillery, 140
1st Massachusetts Sharpshooters, 28
1st Michigan Sharpshooter Regiment, 34
1st Pennsylvania Rifle Regiment, 139
1st U.S. Sharpshooter Regiment, 24, 26, 28, 29, 36, 64, 68, 120, 142
1st Tennessee Regiment, 55
1st Texas Voluntary Infantry Regiment, 11
1st West Virginia Cavalry, 140

20th Massachusetts Regiment, 109
20th Ohio Infantry Regiment, 85, 136
21st Iowa Regiment, 134, 138
21st Mississippi Infantry Regiment, 117
22nd Missouri Volunteers, 138
23rd Georgia, 128
23rd North Carolina, 109
24th South Carolina Volunteers, 73
25th New Jersey Regiment, 128
26th Mississippi Regiment, 139
26th North Carolina, 93
27th Massachusetts Regiment of Volunteer Infantry, 101
2nd Brigade, 2nd Division, 138
2nd Brigade, 4th Division, 139

2nd Brigade, Brown's Division, 139
2nd Georgia Infantry Regiment, 139
2nd Massachusetts Sharpshooters, 28
2nd Missouri Artillery Regiment, 86
2nd New Hampshire Volunteers, 13
2nd U.S. Sharpshooter Regiment, 24, 26, 28, 65, 109, 110, 120, 128, 130, 142
2nd Tennessee Infantry, 55
2nd Texas Infantry, 31
2nd U.S. Artillery, 88

30th Alabama, 141
32nd Indiana Infantry Regiment, 28
33rd Alabama Regiment, 140
33rd Indiana Volunteers, 80
33rd Massachusetts Volunteers, 128
34th Ohio Volunteer Infantry Regiment, 139
35th Illinois Volunteers, 127
36th Illinois Volunteers, 33
37th U.S. Colored Troops, 128
37th Virginia Infantry Regiment, 135
38th Mississippi Infantry, 137
3rd Brigade, 1st Division, 118, 123, 139
3rd Brigade, 2nd Division, 122, 123, 127, 139
3rd Division, 92, 140
3rd Division, II Corps, 140, 143
3rd Regiment, 140

42nd Mississippi Infantry Regiment, 17
48th Pennsylvania Regiment, 140
4th Michigan Regiment, 92
4th Missouri Regiment, 140
4th New Hampshire Regiment, 12
4th Regiment Kentucky Infantry, 103
4th Tennessee Cavalry Regiment, 84, 139

50th New York Engineers, 114, 117
50th Ohio, 93
54th Ohio, 136
56th Volunteer Infantry Regiment, 28
58th Pennsylvania Volunteer Infantry, 139
5th Alabama, 120
5th Arkansas Cavalry, 18
5th Indiana Battery, 118
5th New Jersey Volunteer Infantry, 82
5th Wisconsin, 37

60th New York Infantry, 101
66th Illinois Infantry, 31
6th Mississippi Infantry Regiment, 139
6th Missouri Regiment, 141
77th Illinois Volunteer Infantry Regiment, 139

7th Michigan Regiment, 117
7th Minnesota Regiment, 127
7th New Jersey Volunteer Infantry, 92
7th New York Heavy Artillery Regiment, 140
7th Tennessee Regiment, 48
7th Wisconsin Infantry Regiment, 121

82nd Ohio Infantry, 101
84th Pennsylvania Volunteer Infantry, 138
8th Missouri, 87

9th Corps, 94
9th New York Heavy Artillery, 87

I Corps, 119, 139
II Corps, 130, 131, 139
III Corps, 119
VI Corps, 116, 139
IX Corps, 108, 138, 139
XII Corps, 138
XVI Corps, 127

Abbott, Capt. Joseph, 92
Abbott, Maj. Henry, 88
Abbott, Private Amos, 26
Acton, Capt. Edward, 82
Adair, W.T., 137
Adams, Col. Samuel, 140
Adams, Lieutenant, 90
Adjustable rear sight, 42–43
African American Confederate sharpshooters, 12–13
Albee, George, 67
Andrews Sharpshooters, 28, 36, 63, 88, 129, 130
Andrews, Sgt. William G., 12
Appomattox, 140, 143, 144
Applin, Private Charles, 26
Archer, Brig. Gen. James J., 48
Archer's Brigade, 48
Army of Northern Virginia, 17, 114, 119, 126, 140, 143
Army of the Cumberland, 93
Army of the Potomac, 21, 25, 28, 31, 11o, 114, 119–121, 128, 139
Army of the Tennessee, 54
Arthur, Chester A., 127
Atlanta Campaign, 31, 54, 57, 80, 86, 103, 127, 142

Baker, Col. Edward, 14, 16
Baker, Col. James, 138
Balls Bluff, Virginia, 138
Baltimore Street, Gettysburg, 120, 125

Balzer, George, 58
Barber, Lorenzo, 128
Barker, Lorenzo, 31, 70–71
Barksdale, Gen. William, 114, 117, 120, 139
Barnes, Hosea O., 90
Barry, Brig. Gen. John, 127
Bartleson, Col. Frederick, 140
Bass, Frank, 48
Batchelders Creek, North Carolina, 139
Bate, Maj. Gen. William, 55
Bates, James G., 12–13
Battery Wagner, South Carolina, 102
Battle of Antietam, 36, 65, 109, 110, 114, 121, 126, 128, 138
Battle of Cedar Creek, 87
Battle of Chancellorsville, 61, 98, 100, 126, 128, 138
Battle of Chapin's Bluff, 128
Battle of Cheat Mountain, 9, 138
Battle of Cold Harbor, 94, 101, 139, 140
Battle of Corinth, 31
Battle of Elkhorn Tavern, 16, 33
Battle of Fort Donelson, 30, 82, 92, 127, 138
Battle of Frayser's Farm, 90
Battle of Jones Farm, 94
Battle of Kennesaw Mountain, 93
Battle of Kernstown, 10, 138
Battle of New Market, 29
Battle of Ream's Station, 85
Battle of Sharpsburg, 135
Battle of Shiloh, 15, 55, 128, 143
Battle of Spotsylvania, 80, 87
Battle of Stones River, 92
Battle of the Wilderness, 46, 80, 82, 127, 139, 140
Battle of Wauhatchie, 127
Battle of Williamsburg, 13
Battle of Wilson's Creek, 16, 138
Beard, Private William, 26
Beasley, William, 55
Benjamin, Lt. Samuel, 88
Benson, Berry, 16, 55, 77, 116, 144
Berdan Sharpshooters, 12, 21, 22, 24, 25, 27, 28, 29, 30, 31, 32, 36, 37, 52, 53, 59, 61, 62, 64, 66, 67, 68, 75, 77, 82, 83, 87, 88, 89, 91, 94, 96, 97, 98, 100, 102, 117, 121, 125, 128, 129, 130, 142
Berdan, Col. Hiram, 21, 24, 25, 26, 64, 65, 67, 71, 102, 120, 142
Bethesda Church, Virginia, 140
Betis, Phillip, 58
Bicknell, Capt. Emerson, 130
Birge, Col. John W., 28, 30
Birge's Western Sharpshooters, 28, 30, 70–73, 82
Birney, Gen. David, 126
Black Confederates and Afro-Yankees in Civil War Virginia, 12

Blackford, Maj. Eugene, 19, 125, 129
Blaisdell, Col. William, 140
Bleak House, 88
Boomer, Col. George B., 134, 138
Boone, Lt. Col. Francis, 139
Bowe, Private Prosper, 31
Bowen, Brig. Gen. John S., 142
Bragg, Gen. Braxton, 128
Bragg, Walter L., 15
Branch, Brig. Gen. Lawrence O'Bryan, 138
Bristoe Station, Virginia, 88
British Army, 42
British Pattern 1851, 44
Bronson, Lt. Martin V., 88
Brooks, Capt. T.B., 6
Brown, Col. J.T., 140
Buchanan, Capt. Franklin, 82
Buckbee, Maj. Edward, 34
Burns, John, 121
Burnside, Maj. Gen. Ambrose, 108, 111, 114, 117
Burpee, Col. Thomas F., 140
Burton, James H., 43
Butler, Maj. General Benjamin, 92
Butler, Rev. Francis Eugene 128

Cabell, Gen. W.L., 86
Caldwell, Sgt. Horace, 26
California Joe, 21, 27, 66, 67
Callis, Lt. Col. John, 121
Cameron, Aleck, 137
Cameron, Simon, 24, 67
Camp Davies, Mississippi, 30
Capers, Col. Ellison, 73
Carmichael, Maj. Abner, 93
Carpenter, Lt. Orrin B., 87
Cemetery Ridge, 120, 130
Chamberlain, Maj. Thomas, 121
Chancellorsville, Virginia, 138
Chaplin, Col. Daniel, 140
Chapman, John R., 52
Chapman-James scope, 52
Charleston Mercury, 8, 10, 37, 54, 126, 141
Chattanooga, Tennessee, 111, 127
Cheat Mountain, West Virginia, 138
Chesapeake Bay, Maryland, 28
Chickahominy Creek, Virginia, 94
Chickamauga, Tennessee, 86, 126, 138, 139, 140
Chickasaw Bayou, Mississippi, 13
Chief Nock-ke-chick-faw-me, 34
Civil War Guns, 99
Clay, Henry, 141
Cleburne, Maj. Gen. Patrick, 15, 55

Cobb, Thomas R.R., 16
Collier, Holt, 13
Colt rifles, 65–66
Company K, 34–35, 68
Company L, 28
Constable, Lieutenant Davis, 7
Cook & Brother Manufacturing, 58
"Coonskin Tower," 136
Corrick's Ford, Virginia, 138
Cowles, Brig. Gen. David, 139
Crawford, Charles V., 112
Cross, Col. Edward, 120, 139
CSS *Josiah A. Bell*, 7
CSS *Virginia*, 82
Cumberland Valley, Pennsylvania, 119

D

Dancy, James M., 91
Davidson rifle scope, 49, 50, 51
Davidson, Capt. Greenlee, 61, 75, 98
Davidson, Lt. Col. D., 52, 61
De Monteil, Lt. Col. Victor, 82
"Dead Hole," 141
Decker, John (or George), 15
Deep Bottom, Virginia, 127, 140
Delgadito, 61
Devereux, Maj. J.G., 134
Devil's Den, 122, 124, 125
Dimick Deer and Target Rifles, 30, 70–71
Dimick, Horace, 70
Dodge, Maj. Gen. Grenville, 127
Doles, Brig. Gen. George P., 140
Driscoll, John, 15
Dunlap, Lt. Col. C.W., 134, 138
Dunlop, Maj. William S., 17, 18, 47–48, 77, 83, 117, 143
Durkee, Private Joseph, 37

E

Early, Gen. Jubal, 112
E.H. Rogers Company, 58
Edwards, William B., 99
Elkhorn Tavern, 138
Elliott, Col. Gilbert, 93, 139
Ellis' Ford, Virginia, 101
Enfield rifles, 9, 44, 45, 46, 47, 48, 50, 53, 54
Erwin, Col. Eugene, 139, 141
Ewell, Lt. Gen. Richard, 127

F

Fairbanks, Charles, 24
Falconer, John, 95
False muzzle, 63–64
Farnum, Private Cyrus, 26
Farnum, Private Isaac, 26
Faulk, Capt. W.L., 137
Ferguson, Francis M., 103
"Fighting Parson," 128
Fisch, Robert and Barbara, 47
Fletcher, Private William, 64
Forrest, Gen. Nathan Bedford Forrest, 82, 126–127
Forsyth, Alexander J., 41
Fort Benning, Georgia, 57, 59, 60, 62
Fort Fisher, North Carolina, 95
Fort Loudon, Virginia, 88
Fort Stevens, 112, 113, 117
Fort Sumter, South Carolina, 98
Fort Tyler, Georgia, 140
Fort Wagner, South Carolina, 102
Foster, Rev. Daniel, 128
Foster, Samuel H., 90
Fowler, Lt. Col. Douglas, 139
Fox, Lt. Col. William F., 2, 69
Fox's Gap, Maryland, 108, 138
Frankford Arsenal, 69
Fredericksburg, Virginia, 12, 114, 115, 126, 127
Freemont, Maj. Gen. John C., 30
Fuller, Rev. Arthur Buckminster, 128

G

Garnett, Brig. Gen. Robert S., 6, 9, 138
Garrott, Brig. Gen. Isham, 139, 141
Gascoigne, William, 52
Gettysburg Address, 121
Gettysburg, Pennsylvania, 17, 37, 67, 95, 96, 98, 119–131, 139, 142, 143
Gibbon, Gen. John, 130–131
Gilbert, E.J., 50
Gilmour, Maj. Joseph, 140
Globe Target Sight, 46, 47
Goldsmith, Henry, 103
Goodwin, John, 90
Gordan, Gen. George H., 13
Gordon, Brig. Gen. John, 127
Gough, 2nd Lt. Ben, 98
Granger, Lt. H.H., 90
Grant, Gen. Ulysses S., 30, 117, 126, 133, 134, 136
Graveraet, Lt. Garrett A., 34, 35
Gravis, Captain, 137
Greeley, Corp. A.W., 117

Green, Brig. Gen. Martin Edward, 139, 141
Greene, Albert R., 135
Greene, Brig. Gen. George Sears, 127
Greene, Gen. Nathaniel, 127
Greenwood & Gray, 57
Gresham, Gen. Walter, 127
Greusel, Col. Nicholas, 33
Griffin, George, 91
Griswold, James, 15
Guiney, Brig. Gen. Patrick Robert, 127

H

Haight, James, 142
Haight, Sidney, 142
Haley, John W., 12
Hall, Tom, 7
Halleck, Maj. Gen. Henry, 30
Hampson, Maj. James, 87, 140
Hancock, Gen. Winfield, 98
Hard Grove, 98
Hardee, Lt. Gen. William, 15, 144
Harley, Sgt. Stan C., 15, 52–53
Harper's Weekly, 12, 14, 21, 22, 30, 37, 90, 94, 109
Harpers Ferry Arsenal, 43
Harris, Col. Merry, 139
Harris, Dr. J.V., 96
Harris, F.S., 99
Hatcher's Run, Virginia, 126, 140
Hawthorn, Madison F., 79, 80
Hazel Grove, Virginia, 98
Hazlett, Lt. Charles, 122, 123
Head, Truman "California Joe," 27, 66
Hebert, Brig. Gen. Louis, 141
Heg, Col. Hans Christian, 138, 139
Henderson, Private William, 68
Hendrix, John, 123
Henry rifles, 71–74
Hickok, James "Wild Bill," 33
Hill's Division, 138
Hines, Lieutenant, 91
Hints to Riflemen, 65
Holmes, Oliver Wendell, 112
Holtzapffel & Company, 69
Homer, Winslow, 37, 76, 135
Hood, Gen. John, 102
Hooker, Maj. Gen. Joseph, 109, 110, 111, 126
Hornets' Nest, 15
Howard, Capt. Henderson, 101
Howe, Maj. Shesh B., 140
Hubbard, Capt. W.A., 84
Hurst, Lt. James, 86
Hythe School of Musketry, 54, 83

I

Ide, Private John S.M., 29, 32
Illustrated London News, 111
Infantry Museum, Fort Benning, 59–60, 62
Iron Brigade, 121

J

Jackson, Andrew, 16
Jackson, Henry, Ensign, 82
Jackson, Thomas "Stonewall," 92, 126, 138
James, Morgan rifle, 52, 59, 64
James, Morgan, 52, 59, 64
Jenkins, Brig. Gen. Micah 90
Jewett, Lt. Albert, 12
Johnson, Cpl. Follett, 101
Johnston, Gen. Joseph, 55, 118, 141
Jones, Lt. Col. John Richter, 139
Jordan, Ervin L., Jr., 12

K

Kelley, Andrew J., 95
Kennesaw Mountain, 55, 103, 140
Kentucky Long Rifle, 41, 64
Kernstown, Virginia, 138, 140
Kerr rifles, 15, 55–57, 118
Kerr, James, 55
King, Captain, 95
King, Col. Edward, 139
Kingsbury, Col. Henry, 111
Kirkland, Frederick, 12
Knox, John C., 15
Knox, Thomas, 13
Knoxville, Tennessee, 88, 95, 139
Kreutner, Christian, 58

L

Lainart, Gen. George, 99
Lainart, Lieutenant, 137
Lane, James, 15
Laughton, Capt. John E., 47
Lauman, Col. Jacob G., 30
Lee, Brig. Gen. Albert L., 127
Lee, Gen. Robert E., 9, 16, 17, 80, 107, 108, 109, 110, 114, 119, 120, 126, 138, 140, 142, 143
Lee's Sharpshooters, 18, 83, 117
Leggett, Brig. Gen. Mortiner, 136
Leggett, Maj. Gen. M.D., 93
Legust, D.Y., 137
Lightburn, Brig. Gen. Joseph, 127

Lincoln, Abraham, 14, 24, 25, 64, 65, 67, 112, 121
Lincoln, Mary Todd, 112
Little Round Top, 121–130
London Armoury Company, 56
Longstreet, Gen. James, 88, 90, 102, 111, 120, 121
Lookout Mountain, Tennessee, 93, 135, 139
Lyon, General Nathaniel, 11, 16, 138
Lytle, Brig. Gen. William, 139

M

Magruder, Maj. Gen. John, 10
Maham towers, 83
Mahan, D.H., 135
Mahone, Gen. William, 47
Malcolm, William, 52
Maltby, Private Chauncey, 65
Malvern Hill, 27, 31, 32
Manassas, Virginia, 37, 89
Manchester Ordnance and Rifle Company, 49
Mansfield, Louisiana, 139
Mansfield, Maj. Gen. Joseph K.F., 109, 111, 138
Mantelet shield, 91
Marshall, Col. William R., 127
Mason, Charles, 90
McCarthy's Richmond Howitzwers, 32
McClellan, General George, 11, 14, 25, 28, 31, 32, 33, 67, 108–109, 110
McConnell, Lt. J.D., 85
McCulloch, Gen. Ben, 10, 16, 33, 138
McGowan's Confederate Brigade, 135
McGregor's Artillery Battery, 94
McIntosh, Gen. James, 10
McKinney, John, 15
McKittrick, Capt. Samuel, 98
McKnight, Col. Amor, 138
McMahon, Brig. Gen. Martin, 116
McPherson, Gen. James B., 136
Meade, Gen. George, 119, 120, 126
Medal of Honor, 32, 67, 95, 101, 142
Metcalf, John, 98
Michigan Historical Museum, 71
Miller, S.C., 60
Miller, Lt. J.W., 136
Minie ball, 43–44, 49, 50, 53, 70, 97
Minie rifle, 43
Minie, Capt. Claude-Etienne, 43
Minutes of angle, 97
Missionary Ridge, 126, 143
Mississippi Brigade, 114, 115
Mississippi Rife, 42, 47
Mizer, Sam, 15
Model 1851 Minie Rifle, 43
Moe, Andy, 68

Moore, R.R., 62
Morey, Private Delano, 101
Morris, Col. L.O., 140
Morse target rifle, 58
Mulligan, Brig. Gen. James, 85, 92, 140
Murray rifle, 57
Murray, Col. William, 138
Murray, J.P., 57
Mwa-ke-we-naw, 35

N

National Rifle Association (NRA), 64, 98
Native American sharpshooters, 34–35
Neal, Capt. William, 93
Nesvett, Joseph, 36
New Hope Church, Georgia, 140
New York Herald, 11, 12, 13, 31, 37, 87, 98, 100, 126, 133
New York Post, 26
Newton, Robert C., 18
Nobel, J.C., 59, 60, 62
Norris, Walter, 15

O

"Old One Eye," 35, 141
O'Rourke, Col. Patrick, 125, 139
Orange Court House, 97, 98
Orphan Brigade, 56–57, 81, 118
Osterhaus, Brig. Gen. Peter J., 127
Our Rifles, 98

P

Palfrey, Lt. Col. Francis W., 93
Palmer, Maj. Gen. John, 127
Palmetto Sharpshooters, 6, 90
Park, Capt. Robert E., 112
Patterson, James, 15
Peck, Private Harrison, 64
Pegram, Brig. Gen. John, 140
Pelican, Peter, 33
Pemberton, Maj. Gen. John, 134, 142
Pender, Brig. Gen. William, 101
Pendleton, Gen. W.N., 135
Peninsula Campaign, 37
Periscope rifle, 73
Peters, James Conrad, 82
Petersburg, Virginia, 35, 83, 89, 93, 133, 135, 140, 142, 143
Pickett's Charge, 124, 130
Polk, Lt. Gen. Leonidas, 118
Port Hudson, Mississippi, 139

Porter, Gen. Fitz-John, 31
Post, Col. Henry A.V., 110
Powell, Ben, 55, 116, 117
Prentiss, Brig. Gen. Benjamin, 15, 30
Preston, Theodore, 66
Purdie, Col. Thomas J., 138

R

Ragin, James, 89–90
Rappahannock River, 114, 115, 117
Regimental Losses in the American Civil War, 2, 69
Reno, Maj. Gen. Jesse, 108, 109, 138
Ressacca, Georgia, 126
Red River Campaign, 99
Reynolds, Gen. John F., 119, 123, 124, 130, 139
Rice, Charles, 63
Richmond Enquirer, 80
Richmond, Virginia, 28, 31, 58
Riley, Col. Amos, 140
Ripley, Gen. James W., 65, 66, 67
Ripley, Lt. Col. William Y.W., 29, 31, 32, 36
Roark, Barney, 15
Robb, Lt. Col. Alfred, 92, 138
Rodgers, Anthony, 18
Rogers, Col. William P., 31
Rome Crossroads, 30
Roosevelt, Theodore, 13
Ropes, Private Henry, 117
Rosecrans, Gen. James, 93
Royal Army's 41st Foot, 15
Ruggles, C.L., 136

S

Sabine Pass, Texas, 8
Saller, Lieurgus A., 15
Sanders, Maj. Gen. William Price, 88, 139
Sap roller, 91
Saunders, Captain, 36
Schell, Lt. Abraham "Buck," 15, 55, 57
Scott, Antoine, 35
Second Battle of Bull Run, 82, 92, 127
Second Battle of Winchester, 127
Second Manassas, 126
Sedgwick, Maj. Gen. John, 116, 117, 139
Segrest, Louis, 137
Seminary Ridge, 120, 125
Sepoy Mutiny, India, 61
Seven Days Campaign, 12, 31, 32
Sharps, Christian, 66
Sharps rifles, 27, 66–69, 82, 88, 97, 98, 109
Sharpshooter glasses, 62
Shepard, Irwin, 95

Shepherd, Lt. Col. William, 139
Sherman's March to the Sea, 31
Shiloh, Virginia, 31
Sickles, Gen. Daniel, 61, 126
Simonson, Capt. Peter, 118
Slaughter Pen, 122
Sleeper, Capt. J. Henry, 89
Small, Edward S., 13, 94
Smith, Col. Giles, 87
Smith, Gen. C.F., 30
Smith, Lieutenant, 90
Smith, Maj. W.A., 34
Smyth, Brig. Gen. Thomas, 140, 143
Soldier's Bullet Proof Vest, 96
Spead, Private William, 26
Spencer, Amariah, 71
Spencer, T., 64
Spotsylvania, Virginia, 35, 139
Springfield rifles, 9, 44, 45, 47, 53, 65, 66
Stainrook, Col. Henry J., 138
Stanley, Private Isham, 143
Staples, Sgt. James W., 29
Starnes, Col. James W., 84, 139
Stem, Col. Leander, 92, 138
Stevens, Capt. Charles, 64, 102
Stevenson, Brig. Gen. Thomas, 116, 139
Stone, Col. W.M., 134
Stones River, Tennessee, 138
Strong, Lt. Col. Harrison, 136
Suffolk, Virginia, 11
Sullivan's Island, South Carolina, 83
Sun Tzu, 81

T

Taylor, Captain, 31
Taylor, Col. Charles F., 139
Telescope rifles, 99
Temple, David "Old Dave," 36
Tennessee elevation, 43
Terry, John H.W., 55
The Confederate Veteran, 99
The Improved American Rifle, 52
The Rifle and How to Use It, 65
Thomas Turner Co., 50
Thomas, George "Rock of Chickamauga," 126
Thompson, Ed, 56
Thorpe, Ben, 123
Tichenor, Isaac Taylor, 128
Todd, Alexander, 112
Todd's Tavern, Virginia, 98
Toland, Col. John, 139
Trickett, Charles, 15
True Magazine, 98

Tullahoma, Tennessee, 139
Turner, Capt. Ike, 11
Turner's Sharpshooter Company, 28
Tyler, Brig. Gen. Robert C., 140, 143

U

U.S. Army Sniper School, 57
USS *Clifton*, 8
USS *Monitor*, 82
USS *Morning Light*, 7
USS *Naugatuck*, 7
USS *Petrel*, 7–8
USS *Sachem*, 8
USS *Thomas Freeborn*, 7, 138

V

Vicksburg, Mississippi, 13, 17, 55, 83, 127, 131, 133–144
Vincent, Brig. Gen. Strong, 123, 125, 139
Vinton, Brig. Gen. Francis, 127
Vizetelly, Frank, 111
Volunteer Infantry Regiment, 140

W

Walker, Maj. Gen. William Henry, 140
Wallace, Gen. Lew, 30
Walker, William Henry, 16
Walter Reed Medical Center, 112
Ward, Brig. Gen. John H., 36
Ward, Capt. Robert F., 17
Ward, Com. James H., 7, 36, 138
Warner rifle, 46, 47
Warren, Maj. Gen. Gouverneur, 121, 122, 129
Washington, George, 6, 9. 26

Washington, Lt. Col. John A., 9, 138
Watkins, Sam R., 55
Webb, Lt. Col. Lysander, 139
Weed, Brig. Gen. Stephen, 122, 123, 139
Weller, Jac, 48
Wesson target rifle, 61
West Point, Georgia, 140, 143
West, John, 77, 91
Whipple, Maj. Gen. Amiel Weeks, 61, 98, 138
White, Wyman, S., 34, 65, 69, 94, 117, 128
White House, 112
Whitworth rifles, 15, 46, 48–55, 55, 56, 57, 77, 81, 83, 94, 95, 96, 97–98, 100, 111, 116
Whitworth, Joseph, 50, 97
Wickland, Doug, 98
Wilcox, Brig. Gen. Orlando, 35, 126
Wild Bill, 33
Williams, Captain, 101
Willich, Brig. Gen. August, 127
Winchester rifles, 74
Winchester, Oliver, 74
Winthrop, Theodore, 92
Wister, Col. Langhorne, 121
Wood, Capt. James, 135
Wood, Frank, 123
Worsham, John, 36
Wyman, Col. John B., 13
Wytheville, Virginia, 139

Y

Yorktown, Virginia, 10, 12, 28, 31, 32, 88, 102
Young, Lt. L.D., 118

About the Author

M ajor John L. Plaster, USAR (ret.), served three 1-year tours in Southeast Asia with the top-secret Special Forces covert operations unit, MACV-SOG. Qualified as a Green Beret weapons and communications NCO, he led strategic intelligence-gathering teams deep behind enemy lines in Laos and Cambodia on the Ho Chi Minh Trail. Plaster was wounded once and decorated four times for heroism. Leaving Vietnam as a staff sergeant, due to his extensive combat experience he received a direct commission as a reserve officer.

Combining what he'd learned of stealth, stalking, and camouflage with his postwar experiences as a competitive shooter, in 1983 he cofounded a Reserve Component sniper training program, which quickly became a major national school, instructing hundreds of students from all military services and many law enforcement agencies, including the FBI and U.S. Customs Service. He went on to be a precision rifle instructor at the prestigious Gunsite Training Center, a lecturer for American Special Operations schools, and twice served as Chief of Competition for the U.S. and European military and police sniping championships. In addition to authoring several books—and receiving the Bernal Diaz Award for the best nonfiction military history of 1997—he's designed a specialized sniper rifle stock and other shooting equipment.

In 1998 he was honored as the Special Forces Association's "Man of the Year," and in 2004 was inducted into the Air Commando Association's Hall of Fame. In 2008 he was also inducted into the U.S. Army Special Forces Hall of Fame. Major Plaster has appeared in a dozen documentaries for the *History Channel*, the *Discovery Channel*, and British television, and continues to work on books and firearms-related research.